PRAYER
My Incense to God

PRAYER
MY INCENSE TO GOD

Ramona Freeman

J. Kenkade
PUBLISHING®
Little Rock, Arkansas

Prayer: My Incense to God
Copyright © 2019 by Ramona Freeman

J. Kenkade Publishing
6104 Forbing Rd Little Rock, AR 72209
www.jkenkadepublishing.com

J. Kenkade Publishing is a registered trademark.

Printed in the United States of America
ISBN 978-1-944486-39-6

Let my prayer be like incense offered before you,
and my uplifted hands like the evening sacrifice.
PSALM 141:2 (ISV)

Included in this Book are Prayers on the following topics:

Prayers of Intercession
Prayer for Intercessors
Fourth Watch Prayer
Battle-Ready Prayer for Intercessors

Prayers for Marriage and Family
Decision-Making Prayer for Marriages
Prayer for My Marriage
Prayer for Marriages
Hedge of Thorns Prayer
Prayer for Our Children

Prayers for Spiritual Leadership
Prayer for Our Spiritual Leaders (Broad)
Prayer for Pastors and Spiritual Leadership
Prayer for Spiritual Leaders (Equipping Them in Spiritual Warfare)
Prayer for Spiritual Leaders (Against Worldly Influence)

Prayers for Grief
Prayer During Bereavement

Prayers for Victory Over Circumstances
Prayer for Victory (The Zeal of God)
Prayer for Victory (The Inevitable Defeat of Satan)
Prayer for Victory (Hands Trained for War)
Prayer for Victory Over My Enemy
Declaration of Victory
Prayer to Frustrate the Plans of the Enemy
Prayer to Break Chains of Temptation
Prayer of Freedom from Bondage
Prayer During a Test of Faith
Prayer for Those with Broken and Crushed Spirits
Prayer During Times of Adversity

INTRODUCTION

What is prayer? Prayer is our direct communication line with the Father. It is a dialogue. A conversation. An informal interchange between two or more people in which news and ideas are exchanged. Many have made the concept of prayer complicated and problematic, but it's simple. It's like having a conversation with your best friend. You share your deepest hurts, concerns, and problems while seeking advice and counsel on what to do or how to handle a situation. Who better to run to than the Father? The Creator of all things. The Wonderful Counselor. Our High Priest. Our Advocate. Our Intercessor.

I was introduced to prayer through the most trying times of my life. While struggling for many, many years with rejection, lust, unforgiveness, shame, and hopelessness, and being looked down upon because of my sinful lifestyle by ministry leaders yet still seeking deliverance, I chose to try Jesus Christ. I would spend many hours reading and researching scriptures on things I struggled tirelessly with. I would read books like *The Power of a Praying Woman* by Stormie Omartian and *The Battlefield of the Mind* by Joyce Meyer, along with the Bible, to establish a foundation of prayer and deliverance.

As time progressed, I began to write down prayers using the Word of God, not only for myself but for others as well. I've come to find out that our most essential tool as Christian believers is prayer, not just to change our circumstances but to change *us*.

Through prayer, we invite God into our situations. Jesus has completed His earthly mission and is now seated at the right hand of the Father. He gave us the Holy Spirit so we would have access to Heaven and continue His mission. God is looking for a people who will make up the hedge and stand in the gap before Him (Ez. 22:30). He has placed watchmen on the wall who will cry out to Him day and night, those who will not cease in praying, travailing, and fasting until He establishes every promise (Is. 62:7).

Are you one of His watchmen? Can He trust you to handle the affairs of His kingdom? Will you stand guard and pray the will of the Father through? Are you ready to arm yourself for battle and contend for our nation, for Israel, your children, your health, your marriage, and others? If so, this book is where you want to begin your journey.

These prayers are based on the Word of God. God's Word is true and will not fail. As you pray, remind God of His promises, and, as His Word proceeds from your mouth, be confident that it will not return to Him void. It will be fruitful and succeed in the manner it was sent and declared. Be *blessed.*

Devote yourselves to prayer, being watchful and thankful.
COLOSSIANS 4:2

Prayer for Intercessors

⁓

FATHER, I COME BOLDLY TO THE THRONE OF GRACE that I may obtain mercy and find grace to help me in my time of need. I confess all my sins, those I've committed knowingly and unknowingly and my sins of commission and omission. Your Word states You are faithful and just to forgive my sins and to cleanse me from all unrighteousness. I openly confess my iniquities have made a separation between me and You, God, and have hidden Your face from me so that You cannot hear. I repent and turn to You, Lord, so my sins may be wiped out and I can experience times of refreshing in Your presence. I thank You for blotting out my transgressions for Your own name's sake and not remembering them anymore.

In You, Lord, I have redemption through Your blood and the forgiveness of sins, according to the riches of Your grace. Though my sins are like scarlet, they will be as white as snow. As far as the east is from the west, so far have You removed my transgressions from me. Father, I thank You for forgiving me of my debts, as I have also forgiven my debtors. I'm grateful that, for my sake, God made You to be sin who knew no sin, so that I might become the righteousness of God. I'm grateful that You're not slack to fulfill Your promises as some count slowness, but You're patient towards me, not wishing that I should perish, but that I should reach repentance.

I am overjoyed that there is no condemnation for those who

are in Christ Jesus for the grace of God has appeared, bringing salvation to me. I repent of all wickedness and pray that the intent of my heart be forgiven. May the words of my mouth and the meditation of my heart be pleasing in Your sight, Lord, my Rock and my Redeemer.

Father, I ask that You have mercy on me according to Your unfailing love and, because of Your great compassion, blot out the stain of my sins. Wash me clean, Father, from all my guilt. Purify me from my sin, for I recognize my shameful deeds. They haunt me day and night because I know that I've sinned against You alone and done evil in Your sight. You will be proved right in what You say, and Your judgment against me is always just. I was born a sinner. Yes, from the moment my mother conceived me! But You desire nothing but honesty from my heart, so You can teach me to be wise in my inmost being. Lord, purify me from my sins, and I will be clean. Wash me, and I will be white than snow.

Please give me my joy back! You have broken me, now let me rejoice! Please don't continue to look at my sins. Remove the stain of my guilt. I plead that You'll create in me a clean heart, Father. Renew a right spirit within me. Don't banish me from Your presence, and please don't take Your Holy Spirit from me. Restore the joy of my salvation and make me willing to obey You. Then I will teach Your ways to sinners, and they will return to You.

Father, Your Word says in Ezekiel 36:25-27, "I will sprinkle clean water on you, and you will be clean; I will cleanse you from all your filthiness and from all of your idols. I will give you a new heart and put a new spirit within you; I will take the heart of stone and give you a heart of flesh. I will put My spirit within you and cause you to walk in My statutes, and you will keep My ordinances and do them." I ask that You do it now in my life.

I declare I will follow God's example, as a dearly-loved child, and walk in the way of love, just as Christ loved me and gave Himself for me. There won't be a hint of sexual immorality, or any kind of impurity or greed found in me because they are improper for God's people. There will not be any obscenity, foolish talk, or coarse joking, which are out of place, but rather thanksgiving. No immoral, impure, or greedy person has any inheritance in the Kingdom of Christ; therefore, I avoid these things. No one will deceive me with empty words. Because of such, God's wrath comes on those who are disobedient. I proclaim I will not be in partnership with them. I was once in darkness, but now I am light in the Lord. I will live as a child of light and find out what pleases the Lord. I will have nothing to do with fruitless deeds of darkness but rather expose them. I will be careful about how I live, not as unwise but wise. I will make the most of every opportunity because the days are evil. I will not be foolish but understand what the Lord's will is. I will not get drunk on wine, which leads to debauchery. Instead, I will be filled with the Spirit, speaking to others with psalms, hymns, and songs from the Spirit. I will sing and make music from my heart to the Lord, always giving thanks to God, the Father, for everything, in the name of our Lord Jesus Christ.

God, I thank You for being rich in mercy. You made me alive in Christ even when I was dead in transgressions, for it is by grace I have been saved. I'm grateful You raised me with Christ and seated me with Him in the heavenly realms, in order that, in the coming ages, He might show the incomparable riches of His grace, express in His kindness to me. It is by grace I have been saved, through faith. I realize this is not of myself, but it is a gift of God. It isn't obtained by my works, so that I can boast. For I am God's handiwork, created in Christ Jesus to do good works, which God prepared in advance for me to do.

I pray the God and Father of my Lord Jesus Christ will give me the Spirit of wisdom and revelation, so that I may know

Him better. I pray the eyes of my understanding be enlightened in order that I may know the hope to which He has called me, the riches of His glorious inheritance in His holy people, and His incomparably great power for me. That power is the same as the mighty strength He applied when He raised Christ from the dead and seated Him at His right hand in the heavenly realms, far above all rule and authority, power and dominion, and every name that is invoked, not only in the present age but also in the one to come. God placed all things under His feet and appointed Him to be the head over everything for the church, which is His body, the fullness of Him who fills everything in every way.

I declare Christ has redeemed me from the curse of the law by *becoming* a curse for me, for it is written: "Cursed is everyone that hangs on a tree". He has redeemed me in order that the blessing given to Abraham might come to the Gentiles through Christ Jesus, so that by faith I might receive the promise of the Spirit.

Praise be to the God and Father of our Lord Jesus Christ, who has blessed me in the heavenly realms with every spiritual blessing in Christ. For He chose me in Him before the creation of the world to be holy and blameless in His sight. In love He predestined me for adoption to sonship through Jesus Christ, in accordance with His pleasure and will. Praise to His glorious grace, which he has freely given me in the One he loves. In Him I have redemption through His blood, the forgiveness of sins, in accordance with the riches of God's grace.

I declare, according to the Word of God, that I will be strong in the Lord and in His mighty power. I'm daily putting on the whole armor of God, so I can take my stand against the devil's schemes, for my struggle isn't against flesh and blood, but against the rulers, authorities, and powers of this dark world and against the spiritual forces of evil in the heavenly realms. I put on all parts of my spiritual armor, so that when the day of evil comes, I may be able to stand my ground, and after I have done everything, to stand. I will stand firm, with the belt of truth buckled around my waist, the breast plate of righteousness in place, and my feet fitted with the readiness that comes from the gospel of peace. I have the shield of faith, which extinguishes all the flaming arrows of the evil one. I also have the helmet of salvation and the sword of the Spirit, which is the Word of God. I will continue to pray in the Spirit on all occasions with all kinds of prayers and requests. I will remain alert and always praying for all people.

I will not walk in step with the wicked or stand in the way sinners stand or sit in the company of mockers. My delight is in the law of the Lord. I will meditate on His laws day and night. Consequently, I am like a tree planted by a stream of water, yielding fruit in season. My leaves will not wither, and whatever I do will prosper.

I come in agreement with the Word of God and declare I am blessed in the city and blessed in the country. The fruit of my womb is blessed, and the crops of my land, my livestock, my basket and kneading trough are blessed. I'm blessed when I come in and go out. The Lord will cause every enemy who rises against me to be defeated before me. They will come at me from one direction but flee from me in seven directions. The Lord will send a blessing on my barns and everything I put my hands to. He will bless me in the land He is giving me. The Lord will establish us as His holy people, if I keep His commands and walk in obedience to Him. All peoples on earth will see that I am called by the name of the Lord, and they will fear me. The Lord will give me abundant prosperity in every area of my life. He will open the heavens, the storehouses of His bounty, to send rain on my land in season and bless all the work of my hands. I will lend to many nations but borrow from none. He will make me the head and not the tail.

The Spirit of the Sovereign Lord is on me because He has anointed me to proclaim the good news to the poor, to heal the brokenhearted, to proclaim liberty to the captives and the opening of the prison to those who are bound. I'm anointed to proclaim the acceptable year of the Lord and the day of vengeance of our God, to comfort all who mourn, to preserve those who mourn in Zion, to give them beauty for ashes, the oil of joy for mourning, the garment of praise for the spirit of heaviness so they might be called trees of righteousness, the planting of the Lord, and that He might be glorified.

I boldly confess that I will not be conformed to the pattern of this world but be transformed by the renewing of my mind. Then I will be able to test and approve what God's good, pleasing, and perfect will is.

Lord, open my eyes and turn me from darkness to light, and from the power of Satan to God, so that I may receive forgiveness of sins and a place among those who are sanctified by faith.

I declare I'm sold-out to God, and I yield my members as instruments of righteousness and not of unrighteousness in the name of Jesus. Amen.

Fourth Watch Prayer

FATHER, IN JESUS' NAME, WE ARISE EARLY AND COVER the last watch of the night, setting the atmosphere for our day. We declare all the enemy's plans and strategies for this day will fail. The enemy will not and cannot gain territory in our lives or that of our mates, children, families or friends. Lord, establish the spirit of prosperity and stop the devil from hijacking our blessings and favor. By the power of Jehovah Gibbor, powers, principalities, and all spiritual wickedness are bound and accidents, deaths, thefts, job loss, and any other demonic acts have been cancelled.

You have gone before us to prepare the way, to make the crooked way straight, and to make the rough way smooth. Father, we entrust our work to You. You cause our plans to succeed, and everything we set our hands to do prospers (Proverbs 16:3). Father, today we have favor with all who look upon us, and Your favor makes a circle around us, enclosing us and covering us like a shield. You will work out Your plans for our lives because Your faithful love endures forever.

We enforce Your plans and purpose for our lives against the plans and purpose of Satan. Satan, the blood of Jesus is against you. You have no authority over our lives. No weapon that is used against us will succeed, and anyone who speaks against us will be proven wrong because our vindication comes from God (Isaiah 54:17). You will defeat our enemies; they will come against us but scatter before us in seven directions! (Deuteronomy 28:7).

We declare that today is our day of salvation. Today is our day of deliverance. Today is our day of breakthrough! In the name of Jesus, amen.

(Excerpt from "Watch and Pray: Understanding the Eight Prayer Watches")

Battle-Ready Prayer
for Intercessors

AS YOUR PEOPLE, YOU'VE CALLED US TO ROOT OUT, pull down, destroy, throw down, build and plant. We understand we don't engage in physical battles, but we wrestle "against principalities, against powers, against the rulers of the darkness of this world, against spiritual wickedness in high places" (Eph. 6:12, NKJV). We have spiritual weapons for offense and defense:

The Belt of Truth—Father, we believe the truth of Your Word, for, without it, we will be left vulnerable to being carried about by every wind of doctrine, by the trickery of men, and by the craftiness of people in their deceitful scheming. *But,* because we know the truth of Your Word, we declare we have been made free from the snares of the enemy. We declare Your Word is a lamp to our feet and a light to our pathway. Father, keep us from deviating from the path of righteousness for Your name's sake.

The Breastplate of Righteousness—cover our vital organs and strengthen our hearts against the enemy's attacks. Father, Your Word declares, "We all are as an unclean thing, and our righteousness is as filthy rags". We declare that we walk in righteousness that was purchased for us by Jesus on the cross. We've hidden ourselves in Christ, and, regardless of our failures, His righteousness has been credited to our accounts. Your Word says, "You have clothed us in garments of salvation and covered us with robes of righteousness". Father, protect our hearts and souls from evil and deception.

The Shoes of Peace—change our walk and order our steps. Give us peace that surpasses all our understanding and guard our hearts and minds through Christ Jesus. Your Word says, "Peace I leave with you; My peace, I give to you, and not as the world gives. Let not your heart be troubled, neither let it be afraid". Because we continue to pray and stand in the gap, we know we are continuously under the scope of the enemy. We are continually under attack from Satan. But we are confident of our position in Christ. We will not be moved because we are rooted, grounded, anchored, and secured in You! Father, we dig our shoes of peace into the turf of Your Word, and we declare, "all things will work together for the good of those who love God and are called according to His purpose". This day, we walk in the fullness of the gospel of peace!

The Shield of Faith—we have faith in You, God. We speak to every mountain that has been deceiving and intimidating us, and we say, "Go throw yourself in the sea". We do not doubt in our hearts. We believe, Father, the very thing we speak will come to pass. Your Word says, "whatever we ask for in prayer, if we believe that we have already received it, it will be granted to us". Because we're standing in faith and believing wholeheartedly in Your Word, we can withstand the onslaught of the enemy and render every fiery dart ineffective, unproductive, and powerless in the name of Jesus.

The Helmet of Salvation—we walk in assurance that we are saved by grace through faith. We say thank You, Father, for Your daily protection and deliverance from our sinful nature and Satan's schemes. Through the helmet of salvation, we destroy arguments and every high thing that exalts itself against the knowledge of God, and we take every thought captive to obey Christ. Father, we know our minds are battlefields, and we ask that You renew our minds by the truth of Your Word and wipe out anything contrary to it. Remove old mindsets, ideas, lies, and every bit of confusion. We declare we will no longer be conformed to the pattern of this world but will be transformed by the renewing of our minds so that we can prove what Your good, acceptable and perfect will is. We declare that our protective armor causes our minds to be protected against the illusions, accusations, insinuations, desires, and traps the enemy sets for us. We guard our minds from worldly influences, and we think on those things that are true, honest, just, pure, lovely, of a good report, virtuous, and praiseworthy.

The Sword of the Spirit—we use the Word of God, which is our offensive and defensive weapon against the enemy. Your Word is profitable for teaching, for reproof, for correction and for instruction in righteousness. It is quick and powerful and sharper than any two-edged sword, piercing until it divides soul and spirit, joints and marrow, and it judges the thoughts and intents of our hearts. We believe that, as we declare Your word, it's going into the atmosphere, turning things upside down or right side up, causing situations to change and certain things to come into divine order with the plans and purpose of God. It will accomplish what You desire, and it will prosper in the thing for which it was sent. It will not return void or without results.

Prayer—Father, You commanded us to pray always, with all prayer and supplications in the Spirit, and to be on guard with all perseverance in our prayers for believers everywhere. Father, we use the gift of tongues, and we ask that You help us in our weaknesses because we don't always know what to pray for as we should. We need the Spirit of God to intercede for us with groanings that cannot be expressed in words. Father, we'll pray without ceasing, devoting ourselves to prayer, being watchful and thankful, making sure our armor is intact, and building ourselves up in our most holy faith, as we continue to fight the good fight of faith.

We know: "...though we walk in the flesh, we do not war after the flesh: (For the weapons of our warfare are not carnal, but *mighty* through God to the pulling down of strong holds;) Casting down imaginations, and every high thing that exalts itself against the knowledge of God, and bringing into captivity every thought to the obedience of Christ" (2 Cor. 10:3-5, KJV).

Your Word says, "God resists the proud but gives grace to the humble". So, we submit ourselves to God. We resist the devil, and he will flee from us. We draw near to God, and You draw near to us. We cleanse our hands and purify our hearts, and we will no longer be double-minded" (James 4:6-8, NKJV).

We break every agreement, contract, and alliance we've made with the enemy. We repent right now before You, God. Have mercy on us, O God, according to Your loving-kindness and Your tender mercies that blot out our transgressions. Wash away our iniquities and cleanse us from our sins. We know our sins are always before us, and we've sinned against You. Father, please remember we were sharpened in iniquity. Purge us, Father, with hyssop and wash us, and we'll be whiter than snow. Hide Your face from our sins, O God. Create in us clean hearts and renew right spirits within us. Father, please do not reject us or throw us away from Your presence.

And please do not take Your Holy Spirit from us. Father, restore to us the joy of Your salvation and give us willing spirits to sustain us.

Father, we cover our minds today. We take authority, in the name of Jesus, and destroy every weapon produced against our minds. We demolish every fiery dart and every evil seed planted by the enemy, in the name of Jesus. We take our minds back, in the name of Jesus.

We say NO to:

Nervous Breakdowns	Anxiety	Worry	Stress
Depression	Mood Swings	Confusion	Fear (Phobias)
Hallucinations	Eating disorders	Addictive behaviors	Paranoia
Obsessive disorder	PTSD (trauma)	Insomnia/restlessness	Tourette's syndrome
Dementia	Alzheimer's disease	Schizophrenia	Suicidal thoughts
Homicidal thoughts	Psychosis	Insanity	Delusions
Personality disorder	Developmental disorder	Autism	ADD/ADHD
Fatigue	Narcolepsy	Nightmares	Panic attacks

We declare that we have minds like that of Christ. We cancel every assignment of fear, for You did not give us a spirit of fear, but one of power, love and a sound mind. We defend ourselves against the evil forces of Hell, and we bind them in the name of Jesus. We forbid them to lie to us and use our minds as their playground. We renounce all negative mindsets and all generational curses that may have been passed down our bloodlines. We declare them severed by the powerful blood of the Lamb.

Lord, anoint our minds with the power of the Holy Ghost. Strengthen our inner man with power to fight and war in prayer and intercession. Jehovah Gibbor, go before us now in battle, in Jesus' name.

Decision-Making Prayer
for Marriages

I DECREE THAT MY HUSBAND IS THE HEAD of our home, and he makes sound and wise decisions because he seeks God first. As he seeks God and surrenders to His authority, I submit to him without hesitancy. We will, from this day forward, submit one to another. I declare that my husband values what I say; my opinions and suggestions are weighty to him and his decision-making process. My husband and I resolve important matters quickly. When we are not with one accord, we will seek God in prayer on His directions and guidance about all things, especially regarding our:

- children (discipline, blended families)
- finances (investments and purchases)
- career paths (promotions, relocation)
- religious beliefs

We will not make major decisions in these areas without consulting one another. I rebuke and bind arrogance, pride, big egos, high-mindedness, sarcasm, frustration, confusion, manipulation, domination and disunity. We will remain in harmony, and peace will be maintained during negotiation. We will take the time to weigh the "pros and cons" and share our thoughts, feelings and concerns in a respectful manner and without criticism. My husband and I are always seeking God's guidance and not our own. We will trust in the Lord with all our hearts and lean not on our own understanding. In all our ways, we will acknowledge Him, and He will make our paths straight. I decree that my husband and I walk in unity and are always in God's will. In Jesus' name, amen.

Prayer for My Marriage

DEAR LORD, WE HOLD UP OUR MARRIAGES TO YOU. We understand that marriage is holy. We commit our marriages to You, Lord, that You would cause our thoughts to become agreeable with Your will and we would have successful marriages. Lord, help us to be kind and tenderhearted toward each other, forgiving one another daily, just as You've forgiven us. Father, help us to have hearts of compassion, to walk in humility, and have much patience. We choose to speak the truth in love and listen well to each other. Lord, help us to be quick to hear, slow to speak and slow to become angry. Father, make us strong where we are weak.

Help us to pray together daily and to read and study Your Word together, so we can live in harmony and grow together spiritually. We pray that You be in the midst of our marriage because Your Word says, "A three-stranded cord isn't easily or quickly broken". Father, we declare we will stand the test of time. We will outlast every storm that comes against our marriages. We will survive the winter seasons of our marriages where we experience coldness, harshness, bitterness, hurt, anger, disappointment, loneliness, rejection, discouragement and dissatisfaction. We know that every trial is going to produce patience, patience will produce experience, experience will produce hope, and hope will not make us ashamed because the love of God is being poured into our hearts through the Holy

Spirit, the love that suffers long, is kind, and doesn't envy. It is not boastful or puffed up. It isn't rude or insistent on having its way. It keeps no record of wrongs. It doesn't rejoice in wrongdoing but rejoices in the truth. For the love You give, God, never gives up, never loses faith, is always hopeful, and endures all things.

Lord, forgive us for our selfishness, anger, impatience, vengefulness and foolishness. Father, this day, we put away all bitterness, resentment, animosity, anger, and slander, along with every form of malice. We declare the fruit of the Spirit will be evident in our marriages. Lord, release Your:

love—so we can love without measure despite wrongs, indifferences and offenses

joy—so we can remain in a place of happiness and enjoyment, not because of our mate, but because of You, the center of our joy!

peace—so we can remain calm despite conflicts and disagreements

patience—so we'll be tolerant of each other's imperfections and flaws

kindness—so we'll consider our spouses, their feelings and their needs

goodness—so we can demonstrate good deeds to make each other smile

faithfulness—so we can remain true to our marriage vows: "for better or worse, for richer or poorer, in sickness or in health, until death do us part"

meekness—so we'll be humble and not arrogant or proud

self-control—so we can daily control our mouths, attitudes, and flesh

Father, bring healing to our marriages where there has been infidelity, rejection, misuse of finances, addictions (alcohol, porn, drugs, etc.), and communication barriers. Lord, comfort and mend the brokenhearted, bind up every wound, repair every breach, fill voids as only You can, and deliver us from rejection. Father, You bore our griefs and carried our sorrows, and we declare that, by the stripes and blood of Jesus, our marriages are healed.

Lord, help us to remember that our bodies are not our own—that we belong to each other. We choose not to deprive each other of sexual intimacy and to remain faithful to our mates alone. Father, heal us totally from molestation, rape, incest, sodomy, or anything that would prevent us from giving ourselves fully to our spouses. We declare our marriage beds are undefiled and sanctified. Lord, when facing temptation, You said You'd create a way of escape so we could endure it. We willingly take that escape route, and we say thank You for Your faithfulness and not allowing us to be tempted beyond what we can handle. Lord, we sever every soul tie with past partners with the blood of Jesus. We break the power of the lust of the flesh and the lust of the eye. In the name of Jesus, we rebuke and bind the spirits of perversion, lust, seduction, pornography, incubus, succubus, and every other unclean spirit. And by the blood of the Lamb, we render them inoperable and powerless in our lives.

We resist the enemy that comes to destroy our marriages. We bind the powers of divorce and division, in the name of Jesus. Your powers were broken over two thousand years ago at the cross of Jesus Christ, our Savior. We say no man, woman, demon, or stronghold will be able to separate what God has joined together. Your Word says, "A house divided against itself will not be able to stand". Father, where there is separation, we claim complete restoration for homes, families, and marriages. Holy Spirit, convict our hearts with a deep conviction and deliver us from being defensive, unforgiving, and self-righteous. Your Word says, "The king's heart is like a stream of water in the hand of the Lord; he turns it wherever He wishes". Lord, turn our hearts to You, and those of our spouses and families.

Lord, help us to communicate the truth in love, not offending one another or hitting below the belt. Help us to listen patiently and to respond in a loving manner. Father, even in heated disagreements, help us to never be demeaning or destructive with our words and give us strategies on how to handle not-so-easy situations. Your word tells us, "Be angry and do not sin. Do not let the sun go down while you are still angry and neither give place to the devil". Father, help us to quickly recognize our wrongs and genuinely apologize. We will not go days without communicating or holding grudges. We will not sleep in different beds or leave our homes overnight when having disagreements, for, in doing so, we would give the devil a foothold. In the name of Jesus, we pull down and destroy communication barriers and walls that we've built to protect ourselves from past offenses. Father, help us to communicate in all honesty and respect.

LORD, TEACH HUSBANDS HOW TO:

love us and not be bitter or harsh with us (Col. 3:19)

love us just as Christ loved the church and gave himself up for it (Eph. 5:25)

treat us with consideration as a delicate vessel and show us honor as a joint heir of the grace of life, so his prayers will not be hindered (1 Peter 3:7)

enjoy all their lives with us that God has given them, for this is their reward (Ecc 9:9)

to love us as their own bodies – he who loves his wife loves himself. No man hates his own body, but he nourishes and cherishes it, just as Christ does the church (Eph 5:28-29)

leave their mothers and fathers and be joined to their wives –the two will become one flesh (Eph 5:31)

be sober, worthy of respect, and sound in faith, love, and patience (Titus 2:2)

LORD, TEACH US (WIVES) HOW TO:

be submissive to our own husbands, so that if they are disobedient to the Word, they may be won over without words but by the purity and reverence of our lives (1 Peter 3:3)

be clothed with inner beauty and to possess meek and quiet spirits, which are precious in the sight of God (1 Peter 3:4)

adorn ourselves by being submissive to our own husbands (1 Peter 3:5)

revere (respect) our husbands (Eph 5:33)

submit to our husbands, as it is fitting to the Lord (Col 3:18)

be prudent (understanding) wives (Pro 19:14)

(for older women) be reverent in the way we live, not slanderers, not given to much wine, and teach younger women of what is good (Titus 2:3)

(for young women) love our husbands and children (Titus 2:4)

be self-controlled, chaste, keepers at home, good, obedient to our own husbands, that the word of God not be discredited (Titus 2:5)

be virtuous women:
who know our value is far greater than rubies (jewels).
whose husbands trust in us and see they lack nothing good.
who do our husbands good and not evil.

who are always busy working with our hands.

who rise during the night and provide food for our families

who are knowledgeable in investments and real estate

who are energetic, strong, and hard workers

who extend helping hands to the poor and needy

who are clothed with strength and honor and laugh in the days to come

who speak with wisdom, assuring that the teaching of kindness is on our tongues

who carefully watch the ways of our household and do not eat the bread of idleness

whose children will call us blessed and husbands will praise us

who excel in every area of our lives

who fear God

who receive the fruit of our labor and whose works publicly declare our praise

Lord, surround us with godly counsel. Separate us from those who would seduce us into ungodliness. Help us to remember that evil communication corrupts good manners and character. Give us godly, loving, Christian friends, and a church family. Cause us to hear godly counsel and receive and accept wise instructions.

Lord, thank You for Your faithfulness. Thank You that You watch over Your Word to perform it. Thank You that You are at work within us, causing us to desire and to do Your will. You are the Lord Almighty, and, if You are for us, who can be against us? We love You, Lord, and we entrust our marriages to You. In Jesus' name. Amen.

Prayer for Marriages

FATHER, WE HUMBLY COME BEFORE YOU AND THANK You for saving us from distress when we call out in trouble. Thank You, Lord, for Your kindness, tolerance, and patience with us when we fall into sin, and thank You for sending Christ to die for our sins and redeem us by the cross. We come before You, Lord, to petition You in prayer and ask Your blessing on us and our spouses to come together in harmony with sympathy, compassion, humility, faithfulness, honesty, respect, and, most of all, love. Lord, You have made us one in flesh and spirit. We believe that the Holy Spirit will come upon us, so that we'll never forget Your teachings. Lord, help us to keep Your commands in our hearts. Thank You for Your Holy Spirit working in our marriages. We pray that we will not be deceived by the persuasive words of anyone who would lead us astray or attempt to seduce us.

We give You praise and honor, Lord, and we thank You that no weapon formed against our marriages will be able prosper. With the spiritual authority given to us in Jesus' name, we rebuke anyone who would attempt to put a wedge between us and our spouses through ungodly advice, unwise counsel, or through false teachings or words. Lord, silence the mouths of those who will attempt to come between us, convincing us that reconciliation is wrong.

Lord, we believe the Holy Spirit is working in our spouses' lives right now, ministering to their hearts, convicting and correcting their thoughts, words, and actions. Lord, place in their hearts the burning desire to rebuild our marriages. We bind the enemy and his lies that sometimes tell us the grass is greener in other pastures. We petition You, Lord, that we would humbly accept Your conviction and correction and seek Your direction.

Lord, convict and deal with any unconfused sin in our lives. Help us to deal with any sin that is hindering our marriages. Lord, it's Your desire that we continue to cleave to each other despite anything we've done to each other in the past. Help us to forgive one another unconditionally for wrongdoings. Give us a "let-go" spirit to quickly let go of all offenses, disappointments, failures, and everything that will hinder our marriages.

Father, guard our marriages from infidelity and keep our eyes blinded to temptations of flesh or the influence of the Devil. In the name of Jesus, we pray that You would bind the works of Satan against our marriages. We declare that every plan of the enemy against our marriages is null and void, and we render all of them ineffective.

Lord, we acknowledge You as Lord of our marriages, and we listen to Your still soft voice, as You lead and guide us. Father, we rely on Your strength to keep us strong and courageous during every trial, struggle, and issue. We refuse to be discouraged or defeated. You are the God of all hope, and we claim in every way victory in our marriages. Father, give us new love and appreciation for one another. Where love has died or dwindled, restore it now and allow it to flow genuinely from our hearts without limits or reservation. We will speak the truth to one another in love. Father, help us to honestly share our feelings without being arrogant or spiteful. Father, help us not to hit below the belt. Help us to remember that our fight is not with each other, but with every power and principality that seeks to bring division and chaos. Father, help us to work through all our differences.

We put away all bitterness, wrath, anger, clamor, and slander, along with every form of malice. Instead, we will be kind to one another, tenderhearted and forgiving each other. Father, we pray that You would renew passion and desire between us and heal any emotional wounds we may have caused one another.

It is Your will that marriages be for a lifetime, so what You have joined together, let no man separate. We ask that You protect and defend our marriages and place a hedge of protection over our homes. In the name of Jesus, amen.

Hedge of Thorns Prayer

FATHER, YOU ARE A FAITHFUL GOD, AND I THANK YOU for establishing a hedge of thorns around me and my spouse this day. According to Hosea 2:6-7, You will block the path of the unfaithful with thorns and make a wall, so they cannot find their path. They will pursue their lovers but will not catch them. They will search for them but will not find them. Then they will return to their first spouse.

There are many things the enemy lures us with in our marriage. Father, help us to see the snares of the enemy and to not be ignorant to his devices against us. We know that You are a faithful God, and You will not allow us to be tempted beyond our strength, for, with temptation, You will always provide a way of escape so that we are able to bear it. Help us to always see Your way of escape and to take it, so we are not caught in the traps of the enemy. Father, remove all ungodly desires. I rebuke and bind the spirits of lust, seduction, adultery, fornication, the lust of the eye, the lust of the flesh, and divorce from operating in my marriage. The spirits of jealousy, rejection, pride, rage, discord, addiction, and pornography are bound and declared inoperable in my marriage. Every soul tie between us and any other person, of the same or opposite sex, is shattered by the fire of God. Every generational curse working against our marriage is of no effect, in the name of Jesus Christ, my Lord and Savior.

May my spouse and I lose the yearning to go off-course.

Father, help us to guard our hearts, for out of the heart comes every evil thought (adultery, fornication, and the like). Lord, cause us to return to a covenant relationship with You. Let our relationship with You be our primary concern. Mend our hearts and restore our marriage, which You have ordained. I pray You surround us with grace, patience, and peace and guard our hearts as we wait on You, Lord, to bring this prayer to fruition.

Father, I ask earnestly that You season our speech with grace, so that we will know what, when, and how to respond. Help me to be quick to hear, slow to speak, and slow to become angry. Please flood our hearts with love as to cover a multitude of faults and shortcomings. Lord, create in me and my spouse clean hearts and remove any seeds of bitterness. Grant us grace to forgive and let go of all hurt and disappointment.

Father, set a guard over our mouths and keep watch over the door of our lips. Help us to avoid all evil thoughts and deeds of vengeance against our spouse and to do good towards each other. Help us to seek peace and pursue it and be tools of reconciliation and restoration in our marriage. Reveal to us any act, attitude, or deed acting as a driving force between us. Lord, remove every wedge. Right every wrong. Steer us with Your Holy Spirit and bring us back to You, in Jesus' Name, amen.

Prayer for Our Children

FATHER, WE THANK YOU FOR THE LIVES OF OUR CHILDREN. We thank You for entrusting such great gifts to us, for children are gifts from You. The fruit of the womb is a reward (Ps 127:3). We ask that You give us the love and parenting skills we need to properly teach, discipline, and nurture our children. We declare with confidence the promises of God over our children.

We declare:
the fruit of our womb is blessed (Deu 28:4)
they are blessed and are mighty in the land (Ps 112:2)
they are leaders and not followers; they are fearfully and wonderfully made (Ps 139:14)
the Spirit of God rests upon our sons and daughters – they will prophesy and see visions (Joel 2:28)
they will not depart from the ways or instructions of God because they have been thoroughly trained (Pro 22:6)
they are reared in the nurture and admonition of the Lord (Eph 6:4)
they are not wise in their own eyes – they fear the Lord and turn away from evil (Pro 3:7)
they are the head and not the tail – above only and not beneath (Deu 28:13)

they delight in the law of the Lord and meditate on it continuously. They are firmly planted by rivers of water, producing fruit in its season. Their leaves will not wither, and they will prosper in all they do (Ps 1:2-3)

they will flourish like a palm tree and grow like a cedar in Lebanon (Ps 92:12)

they are taught by the Lord, and great is their peace (Isa 54:13)

they are free from demonic strongholds, generational curses, and hereditary diseases; they are the salt of the earth and the light of the world (Matt 5:13-14)

they are a chose generation, a royal priesthood, a holy nation, a peculiar people (1 Pet 2:9)

they are filled with the spirit of excellence. They will be faithful, responsible, trustworthy. No negligence or corruption will be found in them (Dan 6:3-4)

they will hear and be instructed by the voice of God, and the voice of a stranger they will not follow (John 10:5)

they walk in the Spirit and do not fulfill the lust of their flesh (Gal 5:16)

they hunger and thirst after righteousness and are satisfied (Matt 5:6)

they will let no unwholesome talk, obscenity, foolish talk, or coarse joking proceed from their mouths but only what's useful for building others up (Eph 4:29; 5:4)

they will not be misled – they understand that bad company ruins good morals and character. They will choose wise friends (1 Cor 15:33)

they will prosper and be in good health, just as their souls prosper (3 John 1:2)

they will obey their parents in the Lord (Eph 6:1)

they will be quick to hear, slow to speak and slow to anger (James 1:19) they are protected by God. He watches over their coming out and going, both now and forevermore (Ps 121:8)

they possess power, love, and sound minds – fear has no place in their lives (2 Tim 1:7)

they are strong in the Lord and in the power of His might. They are thoroughly equipped and covered with the whole armor of God (Eph 6:10-11)

they trust in the Lord with all their hearts and lean not on their own understanding. He directs their paths (Pro 3:5-6)

they have the divine protection of God because they dwell in the shelter of the Most High. They are covered by His feathers and, under His wings, they find refuge (Psalm 91:1-2)

they love the Lord with their whole hearts, souls and minds (Mark 12:30)

they walk by faith and not by sight (2 Cor 5:7)

they can and will do all things through Christ, who gives them strength (Phil 4:13)

they will keep the commandments of God, and length of days, long life, and peace will be added to them (Pro 3:1-2)

they possess and display the fruit of the Spirit (love, joy, peace, patience, kindness, goodness, faithfulness, gentleness and self-control) in abundance every day of their lives (Gal 5:22-23)

they are recipients of divine favor, good success, and good understanding in the sight of God and man (Pro 3:4)

they are made in the very image and likeness of God (Gen 1:27)

they are healthy – mentally, emotionally, spiritually, physically, socially, and psychologically; they are protected by God and nothing by any means can harm them (Luke

10:19)

they are blessed in the city and in the country. Every place on which the sole of their feet tread belongs to them (Deu 28:3; 11:24)

they are covered by the blood of Jesus and the angels of the Lord surround them and protect them from all danger

they will find, follow, and flow in the perfect will of God (Jer 29:11)

their steps are order by the Lord and He delights in them (Ps 37:23)

every burden has been removed from their shoulders and every yoke has been destroyed by the anointing of God (Isa 10:27)

they are continually led into victory in Christ (2 Cor 2:14)

they desire the sincere milk of the Word, so that, by it, they may grow up in their salvation (1 Pet 2:2)

they do not love the world nor the things in the world (1 John 2:15)

they are saved by grace through faith (Eph 2:8)

These things we confess by faith over our children. We stand boldly on the Word of God and trust in His promises. They will not return void or empty but will accomplish what You sent Your Word to accomplish (Isa 55:11) The Word of God is living and active (Heb 4:12). It goes before us into the days, weeks, months and years to come. Not one of the Lord's promises will fail concerning our children. Every one of them will surely come to pass (Joshua 21:45).

Prayer for Spiritual Leaders (Broad)

LORD, WE THANK YOU FOR THE SPIRITUAL LEADERS who You have placed on the Earth. Even as they seek Your face to give us, Your people, insight and knowledge that only You can reveal, hold them up now with Your righteous right hand. Lord, allow their generation to line up with what You have ordained. Let the men and women of God that You have selected speak Your oracles. We declare there will be no fear. You have not given them a spirit of fear but love, power, and sound minds. As Your vessels in this earthly realm, there will be no intimidation – allow them to be bold and courageous when declaring Your Word.

Father, give them sons and daughters, both naturally and spiritually, from far off.

Poverty and lack do not have a place in their lives, and they are broken off their ministries.

Let their marriages and family relationships be repaired and restored like new. Lift the heads that hang down low, for You are a shield for them and their glory and the lifter of their heads. Give power to the faint, and to him who has no might increase strength. Let them not abandon their confidence, for it brings a great reward.

We command, in the name of Jesus, that every paralyzing spirit that has a mission to disable Your people from moving forward be bound and cast into the abyss. Through the power of Jehovah Rapha, we rebuke and bind the spirit of infirmity now, in the name of Jesus. Cause Your light to break forth like the morning, Your healing to come quickly, Your righteous to go before them, and the glory of the Lord to be their rear guard. Perfect everything that concerns them. Allow them to throw away the mentality of a hireling and to be the shepherds You have destined them to be, sure to never leave Your sheep astray or away from You.

Your Word declares, "See to it that no one takes you captive through philosophy and vain deceit, after the tradition of men, according to the principles of the world and not God". The spirits of religion and tradition are broken from our ministries this day, and we cast them into the abyss. We decree and declare that Your sons and daughters will not operate in manipulation or control because, by doing so, they open a door to witchcraft.

We declare the spirit of infirmity is bound, in the name of Jesus. We cancel its assignment, and we disallow AIDS/HIV, Alzheimer's, arthritis, blindness, blood clots, brain injuries, brain tumors, every form of cancer, cardiac arrest, deafness, diabetes, fainting, fatigue, genetic disorders, glaucoma, heart attacks, heart diseases, high and low blood pressure, high cholesterol, lung disease, Lupus, migraine headaches, pneumonia, respiratory infections, seizures, strokes, or ulcers to invade the bodies of our leaders.

Lord, You were wounded for their transgressions, and you was bruised for their iniquities. The chastisement of their peace was upon You, and, with Your stripes, they are healed.

Lord Jesus, pour out Your Holy Spirit on those who minister in the ministry of deliverance. May Your power of deliverance work through their hands, as they relieve those affected by demons and captivated by evil spirits, helping free them from Satan's traps, bonds, fetters, and chains. We declare the blood of Jesus is their armor, and it shields them from any and all counterattacks and backlashes of the enemy against their minds, marriages, relationships, children, finances, health, and ministry, in the name of Jesus. Amen.

Prayer for Pastors and Spiritual Leadership

FATHER, IN THE NAME OF JESUS, WE PRAY that the Spirit of the Lord, the spirit of wisdom and understanding, the spirit of counsel and might and the spirit of knowledge will rest upon our pastors, leaders, and elders in our local ministry. Lord, You have anointed and qualified them to preach the Gospel to the meek, the poor, the wealthy and the afflicted. You have sent them to bind up and heal the brokenhearted, to proclaim liberty to the physical and spiritual captives, and to open prisons and the eyes of those who are bound. (Isa 11:2-3) Father, we pray that You will help them prosper abundantly –physically, spiritually, and financially. (Isa 61:1-6; Isa 54:17). They will eat the wealth of the nations. We declare that no weapon that is formed against them will prosper and that any tongue that rises against them in judgment be shown to be in the wrong.

Lord, we thank You that they hold fast and follow the pattern of sound teaching in all faith and love, that is for us in Christ Jesus. They guard and keep with the greatest love—the precious and adapted truth—entrusted to them by the Holy Spirit who abides in them. (2 Tim 1:13,14)

Lord, we pray and believe that daily freedom of utterance is given to our leaders, and they will open their mouths boldly and courageously, as they should to get the gospel to Your people. Thank You, Lord, for the added strength that You have given them, which comes supernaturally. (Eph. 6:19,20)

Father, as prayer warriors, we will stand with them and undergird them in prayer. We will say only good things that will edify and build them up. We will not allow ourselves to judge them but will continue to intercede for them and speak and pray blessings upon their lives in Jesus' name (1 Pet 3:12). Amen.

Prayer for Spiritual Leaders
(Equipping Them in Spiritual Warfare)

LORD, WE THANK YOU FOR THE SPIRITUAL LEADERS who You have placed in the earthly realm. As they seek Your face, Father, release upon them the spirit of the Lord, the spirit of wisdom and understanding, the spirit of counsel and might, the spirit of knowledge and the fear of the Lord. Father, hold them up with Your righteous right hand, and cause them to be servants after Your very own heart. Cause their hearts to be pliable to You, and their ears sensitive to Your voice. Let Your Word be as a two-edged sword in their mouths. May it also be a lamp to their feet and a light to their path. Give them a hunger and thirst for righteousness that only You can fill. By the power and legal authority given to us by Jesus Christ, our Lord and Savior, we reject and denounce the following:

spirit of heaviness
spirit of confusion
spirit of depression
spirit of infirmity
spirit of pride
spirit of discouragement
spirit of oppression
spirit of poverty
spirit of death
spirit of python

spirit of divination
spirit of jealousy
spirit of Anti-Christ
spirit of error
spirit of witchcraft
spirit of whoredom
spirit of bondage
spirit of fear
spirit of rebellion
deaf and dumb spirit
lying spirit
perverse spirit
familiar spirit
seducing spirit

We declare them to be powerless and inoperable in the lives of the men and women of God. We declare they are vigilant and sober-minded, knowing their adversary, the devil, prowls around like a roaring lion, seeking someone to devour. They will continually submit themselves to You, as Lord and Savior of their lives. They will, without fail, resist the devil, and he will flee from them. Father, cause them to be bold and courageous and not afraid or discouraged, for the Lord God is with them wherever they go. You have promised You will never leave, reject, or abandon them.

We declare poverty and lack do not have a place in their lives, and they are broken off their ministries. Father, give them treasures of darkness and hidden riches of secret places, so they may know the Lord, the God of Israel, calls them by their name. Let their marriages and family relationships be repaired and restored like new. Father, be a shield around them, their glory, and the lifter of their heads. When they are weak, make them strong, for You give power to the faint, and to them that have no might You increase their strength. Let them not throw away their confidence, which has a great reward.

In the name of Jesus, we render every paralyzing spirit of no effect. We abort your mission to disable the people of God from moving forward. We declare acceleration to our leaders, ministries, and to the body of Christ. Father, revive and restore life where life has been cut off or stolen. Prune away the old, dead, dried-up areas to invigorate, freshen, revive, and renew their lives, relationships and ministries. Father, repay them for the years the locust, cankerworm, caterpillar or palmerworm have eaten.

Through the power of Jehovah Rapha, we denounce and destroy the spirit of infirmity, in the name of Jesus. Thank You, Father, for the benefits You've given us according to Your Word. We thank You in advance for forgiving the iniquities of our leaders, healing all their diseases, for redeeming their lives from destruction, crowning them with loving-kindness and tender mercies, and satisfying their mouths with good things, so their youth is renewed like the eagles. We thank You that You sent Your Word and healed them, and we can boldly declare they will not die. They will live abundant lives and declare the wondrous works of the Lord. We declare with assurance and in faith that, by Your stripes, they are already healed.

Father, assist our spiritual leaders to throw away the attitude of a hireling and to be good shepherds, as You are a good Shepherd. Give them the grace to stand guard against the enemy when he attempts to attack and scatter Your sheep. Cause them to be men and women after Your own heart and to have a heart of compassion for Your people. Encourage them to not neglect their duties as shepherds when attacks come or when their lives or livelihoods are in danger. Help them to live above reproach, to be monogamous (husband or wife), to be sober-minded, self-controlled, respectable, hospitable, able to teach, not drunkards, not violent but gentle, not quarrelsome, and not lovers of money. Assist them to manage their own households well, with all dignity, and keeping their children submissive, for if someone doesn't know how to manage their own household, how will he care for God's church? Help them to care for, guide, and protect the flock You've entrusted to them, watching over them not out of compulsion, but because it is God's will, not pursuing dishonest gain, but being eager to serve, not lording over them, but leading them example. Help them to give instruction in sound doctrine and to rebuke those who contradict it.

In the name of Jesus, the spirits of religion and tradition are bound, and we cast them into the abyss. The word of God will be declared with clarity, boldness and conviction. The people of God will no longer be conformed to the pattern of this world but will be transformed by the renewing of our minds. Then we'll be able to prove what the good, acceptable, and perfect will of God is. We declare with boldness there will be inward transformation. No itching ears will be soothed. No flesh will be tickled or satisfied. There will be no form of godliness, and we will not deny the power of God to make us holy, righteous, or upright.

We declare and decree their sons and daughters (natural or spiritual) will not operate in disobedience, manipulation or control, for, by doing so, they open the door to witchcraft. We denounce and annihilate all spirits that cunningly desire to oppose and clandestinely overthrow leadership.

Through the blood of Jesus, we come against:
1. The spirit of Korah—the demonic spirit that is birthed through rebellion and stands to oppose the authority of priestly leadership through accusation, disorder and crowd rousing. As

the body of Christ, we are not ignorant to your devices, your persuasion, your charisma and impure motives. Your evil ideas and wicked agendas will fail. The sly and deceitful words you desire to sow into the hearts and mind of others to come against leadership are seedless. In the name of Jesus, we command your works of darkness to cease.

We overthrow your plans, and we declare:
- no longer will you attempt to overthrow the authority God has ordained and establish for this house
- no longer will you cause disruption in the flow or order of ministry
- no more grumbling, murmuring or complaining against leadership
- no longer will you be able to cause dissension, discord or division among the flock
- no longer will your defiance or pride be allowed or accepted but will be judged harshly if not repented of quickly, and
- no longer will there be confusion or perplexity in the congregation.

In the name of Jesus, we pray those who have been influenced by this spirit repent quickly, so they won't experience the wrath of God, just as Korah and his followers did.

2. The spirit of Absalom (the spirit that seeks to scar, ruin, and overtake what God has placed in the Body)— We recognize your works of disobedience, hypocrisy, self-promotion, pride, rebellion, control, jealousy, and resentment against God-ordained authority. Your hidden agendas, strategies, and alliances are of no effect against our spiritual leaders and in the body of Christ. No longer will your intimidation, domination, control, and manipulation succeed. We declare every seed of discord, disunity and rebellion is uprooted and declared seedless and unproductive. Romans 13:2 says, "He who rebels against authority is rebelling against what God has instituted, and those who do so will bring judgment on themselves". Father, reward all evildoers according to their deeds.

3. The spirit of offense and hatred— Father, destroy them. Pluck up every root of bitterness, hatred, and unforgiveness in our hearts. We declare the strategies of the enemy are destroyed through the perfect love of Christ. Because we know that offenses will come, we will be mature and discuss every matter in a calm, healthy manner and not from a wounded place. We will be quick to hear, slow to speak, and slow to become angry. Our words will be as pleasant as a honeycomb, sweet to the soul and healing to the bones. Love prospers in our relationship, and every demonic wedge is removed. Father, help us to freely forgive others for the injustices done to us, and bring healing to our wounded souls.

4. The spirit of Joab, the spirit that seeks to challenge authority and rule and operate in disloyalty and secrecy.

5. The spirit of Jezebel— Father, demolish this spirit that operates in men and women to dominate and control minds, wills, and emotions. Even as Jezebel's mission is to shut the mouths of the prophets, the voice of the Lord shuts down the works of darkness. Every person who has been enslaved by Jezebel's threats and works is free and no longer enslaved.

6. The spirit of Ahab— We bind the spirit that operates silently in Your leaders. They will no longer be passive workers in the Kingdom of God. They will not overlook sin or give up their God-given authority. They will stand and operate in the power and anointing of the Holy Ghost, always fighting the good fight of faith.

Father, raise up the spiritual Jehus in this hour to walk in the power and authority You've given them, for the Spirit of the Living God rests upon them to preach the gospel to the poor, bind up the brokenhearted, proclaim liberty to the captives, and open prison doors to those bound.

Let the fire of God now be released to destroy the works of the spirits of *python* and *Leviathan*. In the name of Jesus, according to Psalms 149:4, You will crown those who are oppressed with victory. Release and vindicate Your people from the clutches of the enemy. Cleanse and remove all wickedness, and let Your anointing destroy every yoke of bondage off Your leaders, in the name of Jesus. Amen.

Prayer for Spiritual Leaders
(Against Worldly Influence)

⁓

WE LAY AN AXE TO THE ROOT OF THE DEVIL'S PLAN to steal, kill, and destroy our ministry leaders. We say NO to:

untimely deaths
adulterous affairs
criticism, insensitivity from members, leadership or co-laborers
sabotage, backbiting
lies, accusations, gossip, slander, misrepresentation, reproach
violence, drugs and alcohol abuse
depression and suicidal thoughts
sickness, poor health
spiritual death
severed relationships
struggle of balancing home, life and ministry
pressure of perfections
all demonic attacks against their lives, marriages, children, ministry, health, finances, and minds.

This day, we pull down strongholds, casting down arguments and every high thing that exalts itself against the knowledge of

God, bringing every thought into captivity to the obedience of Christ.

We say NO to:
guilt, shame and condemnation
silent struggle
being overwhelmed
chemical imbalances and mental illnesses
burnout
disappointments
betrayal

Prayer During Bereavement

Father, Your Word declares, "For everything there is a season, and a time for every matter under heaven: a time to be born, and a time to die; a time to plant, and a time to pluck up what is planted; a time to kill, and a time to heal; a time to break down, and a time to build up; a time to weep, and a time to laugh; a time to mourn, and a time to dance" (Ecc 3:1-8).

We know that You are the same God in the valley as on the mountaintop. Father, comfort my family once again during this time of mourning and weeping, as another family member has been plucked from this earthly realm. Isaiah 53:4 says, "[You] bore our griefs and carried our sorrows". Father, heal the broken hearts of the spouse, children, siblings, friends, and family of our loved one and bind up their wounds.

I pray that Your everlasting joy will cover their heads and gladness will cause sorrow to flee. We declare, even in this, You are to still be glorified! For our loved one's body has been transformed from perishable to imperishable, from mortal to immortal. For it is written, "Death is swallowed up in victory! O death, where is your sting? O death, where is your victory?" We're confident and pleased to say that to be absent from the body is to be present with the Lord.

Prayer for Victory
(The Zeal of God)

MAJESTIC CREATOR, EVERLASTING FATHER, we rest assured that all our days are held in Your hand, crafted into Your perfect plan for us. As we give our hearts to You today, Lord, open our minds, bodies, and souls to receive the inflow of great wisdom of Your Word and overflowing, unspeakable joy. We thank You for all You've done for us, and we praise Your Holy Name. Lord, nothing is hidden from You, for the eyes of the Lord move to and fro throughout the whole earth to show Himself strong on behalf of those whose hearts are blameless to Him. You know our hearts and what we desire. Your eyes see both good and evil in the land.

Father, You and Your angels battle on our behalf when our hearts are focused on You and You alone. You are always on our side. The Lord is a man of war. He will go forth as a mighty man. He will stir up His zeal like a man of war. He will cry. Yes, roar! He will prevail and triumph over our enemies.

Life consists of many battles, but, for us, only victory lies ahead! Thanks be to God, our Father, who gives us victory through Jesus Christ, our Lord, and who always causes us to triumph.

Father, help us fight against the evil spirits of this world. The devil's army increases daily, but we clothe ourselves with the full armor of God. We charge into battle, confident that the battle has already been won at the cross. We bind every demonic force, the prince of the power of the air, along with his minions and imps. We declare by faith and with the authority the Father has given us, they will not prevail against us! Every attack against our finances, our health, our minds, our relationships, our marriages, our children, and our joy will not prevail! Hallelujah!

Jesus, Your Holy Spirit dwells within us. Prayer and Your Word carry us through to victory! We are crucified with Christ! We declare today that we are victorious, and we take dominion over the devil and his lies through Jesus Christ, our Lord and Savior! Victory is ours! In Jesus' mighty name, amen!

Prayer for Victory
(The Inevitable Defeat of Satan)

BY THE POWER AND AUTHORITY GOD HAS GIVEN ME
in His name, I command you, Satan, to cease all your activities
against me, my spouse, children, family, friends, acquaintances,
and brothers and sisters in Christ. I bind you and all your
seedings, works, plans, and activities at their roots. I pull down
your every stronghold, in the name of Jesus.

I don't come on my own accord but in the name of Jesus,
fully clothed with the whole armor of God. I put on the girdle
of truth, the breastplate of righteousness, the sandals of peace,
and the helmet of salvation. I lift the shield of faith against all
the fiery darts and take in my hand the sword of the spirit, the
Word of God. The weapons of our warfare are not carnal but
mighty through God to pull down strongholds, to cast down
imaginations and every high thing that exalts itself against the
knowledge of God, and to bring every thought into obedience
to the Lord, Jesus Christ.

In Jesus' name, I come against every principality, every
demonic spirit, and every act of spiritual wickedness in high
places. I seal your spirit-lips shut by the power and might of
the Holy Spirit. Every line of communication that you use to
deceive God's people is severed. We will not be deceived by
what we see, by our feelings or emotions. We walk by faith and
not by sight. On this day we choose to believe the report of the

Lord. I plead the precious Blood of Jesus over every person that I'm connected to, from the top of their head to the soles of their feet, and I decree that you can't touch us, and you can't have us! Get your hands back! Get out!

Because I have the Greater One inside of me, I have power and authority to trample over serpents and scorpions and over all your power. I decree all your tactics are trampled and cut down, and all your plans against my family and God's people are cancelled, made null and void, never manifested, never come to pass, cursed and destroyed at their roots, and rendered of no effect, in Jesus' Name! Amen!

Prayer for Victory
(Hands Trained for War)

FATHER, WE THANK YOU THAT VICTORY IS PROMISED to us through Jesus Christ, our Lord. This day we clothe ourselves with the whole armor of God, that when the evil comes, we'll be able to stand our ground against the enemy (Eph 6:13). We submit ourselves to You, God, and we thank You that the enemy flees from us (James 4:7). For the Lord our God walks in the midst of us to deliver us and hand our enemies over to us (Deu 23:14).

Thank You Father for giving us divine authority to trample on serpents and scorpions, and over all the power of the enemy and nothing will be able to harm us (Luke 10:19). We boldly declare, no weapon the enemy forms against us, our children, our marriages, our ministry, and our nation will prosper. Every tongue that rises against us in judgment we condemn now, for this is the heritage of the servants of the Lord (Isa 54:17). It's through Jehovah Gibbor we push down our enemies. It's through Your name we trample those who rise against us, for our trust isn't in our bow or sword to save us, but You save us from our enemies and have put to shame those who hate us (Ps 44:5). We confess no man will be able to stand before us all the days of our lives, for as You were with our forefather, Moses, so will You be with us. Lord, You promised to never leave or forsake us (Jos 1:5).

Blessed be the Lord, our Rock, who trains our hands for war and our fingers for battle. We boldly confess that You are our fortress, our high tower, our deliverer, and our shield (Ps 144:1). For by You we can run through troops and leap over walls (2 Sam 22:29). It is God who arms us with strength and makes our way perfect. It is He who makes our feet like the feet of deer and sets us on high places. He teaches our hand to make war, so that our arms can bend a bow of bronze. We will pursue every enemy and overtake them. We will not turn back until they are destroyed, wounded, and never to arise, for You have armed us with strength for battle (Ps 18:32-39).

The Lord is our strength and shield (Psalm 28:7). He is our rock, our fortress and our deliverer, the God of our strength. In Him we trust, our shield, the horn of our salvation, our stronghold, our refuge, and our Savior (2 Sam 22:2). He will deliver us from every evil work and preserve us (2 Tim 4:18). He will hide us in the secret place of His presence from the plots of man, and He will keep us secretly in a pavilion from the strife of tongues (Ps. 31:19). When the wicked come against us to eat up our flesh, our enemies and foes, they will surely fall. Though an army encamps around us, our hearts will not fear; though war rises against us, in this, we will be confident (Ps 27:2-3).

The Lord is a Man of War. The Lord is His name (Ex 15:3). He will go forth like a mighty man. He will stir up His zeal like a Man of War (Isa 42:13). He goes before us as a consuming fire. He destroys our enemies before us, so we can drive them out and destroy them quickly (Deu 9:3). He will guard the feet of His saints, but the wicked will be silent in darkness. For by strength no man will prevail. The adversaries of the Lord will be broken in pieces (1 Sam 2:9-10). We will not be afraid because of this great multitude, for the battle is not ours, but God's. We will not need to fight in this battle. We position ourselves, stand still, and see the salvation of the Lord (2 Chr 20:15-17). We declare by faith: VICTORY IS MINE! In Jesus' name, amen.

Prayer of Victory Over My Enemy

FATHER, YOU HAVE GIVEN US THE KEYS to the Kingdom to bind and loose. We use those keys to bind, unlock, break, and smash everything that has hindered us from fulfilling Your perfect plans for our lives. We decree and declare that every chain, rope, bar, and fetter is loosed, broken off, and removed from our lives in Jesus' name. Father, we thank You that You alone are the judge over our lives. According to Your word, the heart is deceitful, above all things, and desperately wicked. Who can know it? You, Lord, search the heart, try the reins, even to give every man according to his ways, and according to the fruit of his doings.

Father, in Jesus' name, Your Word tells us to fear not, for You are with us. We will not be discouraged, for You are our God. You will strengthen us, help us, and uphold us with Your righteous right hand. All those who plotted against us will be confounded and ashamed. They will be as nothing. Father, we stand in agreement with Your Word of power, strength, assurance, and confidence that You will protect us from the enemy. You told us that vengeance is Yours and You will repay the evil ones. Lord, we praise You and thank You, for Your protection and Your Word of power and deliverance.

Father, You said in Your Word that You would keep evil

men from carrying out their plans against us. Father, we take authority of Your Word, and bind, cancel, and uproot all evil plans of the enemy, in Jesus' name.

We declare that, "When the wicked, even our enemies and our foes, come upon us to eat up our flesh, they will stumble and fall". When the enemies come to eat up our flesh, when we're vulnerable, weak, spiritually asleep, and discouraged, the power in the blood of Jesus will be a shield for us. Thank You, Lord for Your protection. Thank You, Lord, that You are watching over us.

Declaration of Victory

I DECLARE THAT TODAY MARKS THE END of a sad, depressing, discouraging past and the *beginning* of a prosperous, joyous, debt-free, disease-free, depression-free future. The remainder of this year is pregnant with and will birth my purpose, promise, and potential. It will bring forth *divine* opportunities that I will discern and take full advantage of. It will be filled with wonderful surprises, supernatural breakthroughs, and astounding miracles. I will be empowered to accomplish that which I was born to do, and I will become all that I was born to be. I will not live a mediocre life but one of victory, triumph, and God-success. My victories are as abundant as grains of sand. All that was lost has been restored because *greatness* is my portion. In Jesus' name. Amen.

Prayer to Frustrate the Plans of the Enemy

THE LORD FRUSTRATES THE COUNSEL of the nations. He restrains the purpose of the people (Psalms 33:10). He frustrates the plans, schemes, and devices of the crafty, so that their hands cannot accomplish what they plan (Job 5:12). So, we say to our enemy to devise a plan, but it will fail and come to nothing. Speak a word, and it will not stand, for God is with us (Isaiah 8:10).

Father, expose the false prophets as liars; cause the omens of boasters to fail and make fools out of diviners. Confound the wise and make their knowledge foolish (Isaiah 44:25).

...for the counseling of the Lord will stand (Proverb 19:21).

... He will accomplish all for His pleasure and purpose (Isaiah 46:10).

Prayer to Break Chains of Temptation

HELP US FATHER, TO BREAK THESE CHAINS OF TEMPTATION. Tear down these strongholds that are weakening us. We rebuke and bind every evil spirit that attempts to lure us into the abyss. Father, we declare we are strong in the Lord and in the power of His might. We put on the whole armor of God, so we can stand against the devil's schemes, tricks, and enticements. Lord, lead us, guide us, walk beside us, so that we may not stray or fall by the wayside but if we do, Lord, please pick us up and hold us in Your loving arms. Thank You for being faithful and not allowing temptation to be more than we can stand. Thank You for creating a way of escape for us. We recognize it and take it. We submit ourselves to You this day. We resist the devil, and he flees from us.

Father, help us to continue to be vigilant and sober-minded, knowing we have an adversary, the devil, that consistently prowls around like a roaring lion looking to devour us. This day, we walk in the Spirit and will not fulfill the lust of our flesh. We make no provision to satisfy the fleshly desires. We put on the new man created in righteousness and true holiness.

This day, we declare, sin has no power over us. No longer do we yield our bodies as instruments of evil to serve sin but as instruments of *righteousness* to God, our Father. In Jesus' name, amen.

Prayer of Freedom from Bondage

WE WILL STAND FAST IN THE LIBERTY through which Christ has made us free and will not be entangled again with the yoke of bondage (Gal 5:1). We declare with boldness that whom the Son sets free is free indeed (John 8:36). We are free, and no more chains are holding us! We declare every bondage and demonic stronghold is broken off our lives. We shake ourselves from the dust and rise up. We loose ourselves from the chains around our necks (Isa 52:2). Father, loose the bands of wickedness, undo every heavy burden, let the oppressed go free, and break every yoke (Isa 58:6).

The Spirit of the Lord God is upon us because the Lord has anointed us to preach good news to the meek. He has sent us to bind up the brokenhearted, to proclaim liberty to the captives, and the opening of the prison to them that are bound (Isa 61:1). So, we say to the captive, "Come out", and to those in darkness, "Come into the light and be free" (Isa 49:9). For we were bought with a price, so we glorify God in our body and spirit, which are God's (1 Cor 6:20). Our body is a temple of the Holy Spirit within us, whom we have from God. We are not our own (1 Cor 6:9). We come out from among unbelievers and separate ourselves (2 Cor 6:17). For we are a chosen generation, a royal priesthood, a holy nation, a peculiar people that You have called out of darkness into the marvelous light (1 Pet 2:9).

We will not be unequally yoked together with unbelievers, for righteousness and unrighteousness have no fellowship, and light and darkness have no communion, nor Christ with Belial or a believer with an unbeliever. There's no agreement with the temple of God and idols. We boldly confess that the Lord God lives and walks in us. He's our God, and we are His people (2 Cor 6:14-16).

Prayer for Prosperity

MY GOD WILL SUPPLY ALL MY NEEDS according to his riches in glory by Christ Jesus, for He's my shepherd, and I want for nothing (Phil 4:19; Ps 23:1). Father, we've obeyed Your commandments regarding tithing and giving. You commanded us to bring all the tithes into the storehouse, so there will be meat in Your house. You told us to put You to the test and You would give us a seven-fold blessing, that You would:

> open the windows of heaven,
> pour out a blessing that there will not be room enough to receive,
> rebuke the devourer for my sake,
> not destroy the fruits of my ground,
> not allow my vine to cast its fruit before time,
> make sure all nations will call me blessed,
> make me a delightsome land (Mal 3:10-12).

We rejoice in the Lord, our God, because He has given us the former rain moderately. He will cause the former rain and the latter rain in the first month. The threshing floor will be filled with grain. Our vats will overflow with new wine and oil. And He will restore to me the years the locust, cankerworm, caterpillar, and palmerworm has eaten (Joel 2:23-25). My God supplies seed to the sower and bread for food. He supplies and multiplies my seed for sowing and increases the harvest of my righteousness. Amen.

Prosperity Declaration

I AM A MILLIONAIRE! I AM NOT A BORROWER but a lender to many. I will lack no good thing because I serve the Lord and walk upright. The blessings of the Lord make me rich and add no sorrow. Because I'm a tithe-payer and a seed-sower, the windows of heaven have been opened over my life. I have so much that I don't have enough room or space to contain it! For my God has blessed me with exceedingly-abundantly-pressed down-shaken together-running-over blessings! Jehovah Jireh has blessed me with treasures of darkness and hidden wealth of His secret place. He has caused the wealth of the wicked to be transferred into my hands and in my possession. My trust and hope are in the Lord.

Therefore, I am like a tree planted by the water, and my roots extend by the river. I will not fear when the heat comes; my leaves will remain green, and I will not be anxious or worry in a year or time of drought, nor will I cease to yield or produce fruit. My God gives me the power to get wealth, witty inventions, financial strategies, and clever ideas in order to fulfill the covenant He confirmed to my forefathers.

I thank the Lord of Hosts for rebuking the devourer for my sake; he cannot destroy the fruits of my ground, neither will my harvest manifest before God's appointed time. All nations will call me blessed because I am a land of delight!

Prayer for Healing and Deliverance

HEAVENLY FATHER, WE COME INTO YOUR PRESENCE in the name of Jesus. Your word says, "Where two or more are gathered in My name, there I will be in the midst". We enter Your gates with thanksgiving and enter Your courts with praise! You are wonderful and powerful, Father, and You are worthy of all praise. We bless You, Lord, and with all that is within us, we bless Your holy name. We believe in Your Son, Jesus, who is the way, the truth and the life, and we accept Your gift of salvation through Him. And because we are saved, we lay claim to the benefits and promises of healing and deliverance.

Psalm 103:1-3 says, "You have given us benefits. You have forgiven us for all our iniquities; You healed us from all our diseases. You redeemed our lives from destruction. You've crowned us with lovingkindness and tender mercies".

Psalm 118:17 says, "We will live and not die and declare the wondrous, amazing, and incredible acts of the Lord".

Psalm 147:3 says, "He heals the brokenhearted and binds up their wounds (curing their pains and their sorrows)".

Psalm 30:2 says, "I cried out to You, O Lord, and You saved me and healed me".

Father, You kept Your word to us and gave us Your very best, Your only son. And because we believe in Him, we will not perish or see eternal death, but we have everlasting life.

Isaiah 53:4-5 and 1 Peter 2:24 say, "He was wounded for our transgressions, bruised for our iniquities, and the chastisement of our peace was upon him, and by His stripes, we are already healed".

Ephesians 1:7 says, "We have redemption through the blood of Jesus Christ, our Lord and Savior".

Psalm 107:2 says, "We boldly declare we have been redeemed from the hand of the enemy". The enemy has absolutely no authority in our lives at all unless we give him a foothold (Eph 4:27). And we refuse to give him a footing into our lives.

James 4:7 says, "Submit yourselves to God, resist the devil, and he will flee from you". This is what we choose to do right now by Your grace.

We come to You today, Father, in the name of Jesus Christ. Help us to present our bodies as living sacrifices and renew our minds by the Word of God, so that we may experience Your good, acceptable, and perfect will (Rom 12:3).

In the name of Jesus and through the blood and authority of Jesus Christ, we say to the enemy: "We command all evil spirits in our lives and in the lives of our loved ones that are causing tension, strife, disagreement and sickness in our minds and bodies, and any evil spirits that are blocking or hindering the free-flow of the glory of God in our lives to stop right now and be removed and be cast out, in the name of Jesus" (Matthew 21:21).

Jesus told us in Matthew 16:19 that He gave us the keys to the Kingdom of Heaven. Whatever we bind on earth will be bound in heaven, and whatever we loose on earth, will be loosed in Heaven. In Matthew 8:16-17, many were under the power of demons, and Jesus drove out the spirits with a word and restored to health all who were sick. To borrow the words of Isaiah, "He took our weaknesses and infirmities and bore away our diseases".

We bind all the power of the enemy trying to operate in our lives and in the lives of all our loved ones. We loose into our lives the mighty power of the Living God, El Shaddai, the All-Sufficient, and Almighty God through grace by our strong faith in Jesus' finished work on the cross. Father, we receive Your Almighty power flowing in our lives and in the lives of our families, friends and loved ones and declare the power of God is hindering, stopping, and driving away all demonic spirits!

FATHER, BREAK EVERY GENERATIONAL CURSE OF:

Lust	Perversion	Uncleanness	Impurity
Adultery	Fornication	Rape	Molestation
Sorcery	Divination	Hatred	Anger
Revenge	Retaliation	Bitterness	Pride
Disobedience	Rebellion	Jealousy	Covetousness
Unbelief	Doubt	Destruction	Murder
Poverty	Lack	Divorce	Separation
Confusion	Mental illness	Schizophrenia	Discouragement
Rejection	Deception	Shame	Condemnation
Infirmity	Addiction to drugs, alcohol, illegal substances, sex, etc.	Witchcraft	Whoredom
Arrogance	Fear	Violence	Double-mindedness
Sickness	Resentment		

FATHER, BREAK THE POWER OF THE SPIRIT OF INFIRMITY THAT ATTEMPTS TO ATTACH ITSELF TO OUR BODIES AND MANIFEST ITSELF IN:

Cancer: lungs, bones, breast, throat, back, spine, liver, kidneys, pancreas, skin or stomach					
Diabetes	High blood pressure	Low blood pressure	Heart attack	Stroke	Kidney failure
Leukemia	Blood disease	Breathing problems	Arthritis	Lupus	Alzheimer's
Insomnia	Aneurysm	Brain tumors	Asthma	Allergies	Seizures
AIDS/HIV	Blindness	Glaucoma	Down syndrome	Sickle cell	Lung disease
Crib deaths	Deafness	Fever	Pneumonia	Ulcers	Fainting
Fatigue	High cholesterol	Migraine headaches	Stillborn pregnancies	Flu	Thyroid problems
Sinus infections	Staph infections	Respiratory infection	Blood clots		
Mental Disorders: Anxiety disorder, Bipolar, Major Depressive, Eating disorder, Panic, Postpartum Depression, Post Traumatic Stress Disorder (PTSD), Nightmare, Narcolepsy, Suicidal/homicidal thoughts					
Learning Disorder: ADHD/ADD, Autism, Mental Retardation, Intelligence Delay					

WE PLEAD THE BLOOD OF JESUS OVER OUR ENTIRE BODIES AND COMMAND OUR BODIES AND SYSTEMS TO PERFORM TO THE PERFECTION THAT GOD CREATED THEM TO FUNCTION.

WE SPEAK LIFE TO OUR:

Circulatory system - consists of the heart and a network of vessels that carry blood. It supplies oxygen and nutrients to the body's cells and removes waste products.	Heart, blood vessels, blood, capillaries and veins
Digestive system - takes in food the body needs to fuel its activities. It breaks the food down into units called nutrients and absorbs the nutrients into the blood.	Esophagus, stomach, liver, gall bladder, large/small intestines
Endocrine system - provides chemical communication within the body using hormones	Pituitary glands, thyroid glands, adrenal glands, pancreas, testes
Exocrine system - protects the body's internal parts from damage and provide a barrier to invasion by infectious organisms.	Skin, hair, sweat and nails
Lymphatic system- a network of vessels that collects fluid from tissues and returns it to the blood. It also contains groups of cells that protect the body against infections.	Lymph nodes, tonsils, thymus, spleen
Muscular system - consists of layers of muscles that cover the bones of the skeleton, extend across joints, and can contract and relax to produce movement.	Skeletal muscles and tendons
Nervous system - the body's main control system.	Brain, spinal cord, and a network of nerves that extend out to the rest of the body.
Renal system/Urinary system - system where kidneys filter blood	Kidneys, urinary bladder, ureters, and urethra
Respiratory system - is centered on the lungs, which work to get life-giving oxygen into the blood. They also rid the body of a waste product, carbon dioxide.	Lungs, pharynx, larynx, trachea, bronchi, lungs and diaphragm
Skeletal system - a strong yet flexible framework of bones and connective tissue. It provides support for the body and protection for many of its internal parts.	Cartilage, bones and joints
Reproductive system - the male and female parts produce the sperm and eggs needed to create a new person. They also bring these tiny cells together.	Penis, testes ovaries, uterus vagina

We declare it is finished! It is done! We believe the Word of God wholeheartedly and declare it is so! In Jesus' name we pray, amen.

Prayer During a Test of Faith

FATHER, WE COUNT IT ALL JOY WHEN WE FALL into diverse temptations, knowing that the trying of our faith produces patience. We will let patience have its perfect work, that we may be perfect and whole, wanting nothing (James 1:2-4). We boldly declare with assurance, that after we have suffered a while, You will make us perfect, established, strengthened, and settled (1 Pet 5:9). We will not lose heart, though our outer man is decaying, and our inner man is being renewed day by day. By faith we know our light affliction, that is for a moment, works for us a far more exceeding and eternal weight of glory (2 Cor 4:16-17). For Your Word says, "...weeping may endure for a night, but joy comes in the morning" (Ps 30:5). We declare that our night is over, and morning has come!

We are heirs of God and joint-heirs with Christ. If we suffer with Him, we will be also glorified together. We consider that the sufferings we are experiencing are not worth comparing to the glory that will be revealed in us (Rom 8:17-18). We will not think it strange concerning the fiery trials that have come to us, as though some strange thing has happened to us; instead, we rejoice that we are partakers of Christ's sufferings. So, when Your glory is revealed, we will be glad, with exceeding joy (1 Pet 4:12-13). We greatly rejoice that for a season we have had to suffer grief in all kinds of trials. The trial of our faith, being much more precious than of gold that perishes, though it be tried with fire, might be found to praise, honor, and glory (1 Pet 1:6-7).

Prayer for Those with Broken and Crushed Spirits

FATHER, THANK YOU FOR YOUR WORD in Psalm 34:18, which says, "The Lord is near to the brokenhearted and saves those who are crushed in spirit". I declare, "The Spirit of the Lord is upon me because He has anointed me to preach the gospel to the poor. He has sent me to heal the brokenhearted, to preach deliverance to the captives and recovery of sight to the blind, to set at liberty those who are oppressed…" Father, I stand in the gap for my dear friend. I ask that You mend their broken heart and bind up every wound. I rebuke, bind, and reject:

    all emotional wounds (physical, mental, verbal, and sexual)

    abandonment

    broken relationships (with children, siblings, parents, divorce, etc.)

    low self-esteem and self-pity

    anger, bitterness, hate, and violence

    eating disorders (anorexia, bulimia, binge-eating, etc.)

    insomnia, worry, anxiety, and stress

    shame, guilt, condemnation and unworthiness

    oppression, depression and suicidal thoughts

    effects of past sins (abortions, failed marriages,

adultery, addictions, etc.)
deep-seated grief and sorrow
fatigue (mental, spiritual, emotional and physical)

Father, renew them with Your strength, so that they can soar with wings as eagles, as written in Isaiah 40:31. Father, do not allow them to become weary or faint. Restore their mental, spiritual, physical, and emotional health and well-being. Heal them of insomnia, so that they can sleep peacefully throughout the night. I pray that, from this day forward, they will lie down and sleep in peace, for You alone make them to dwell in safety (Psalm 4:8).

Empower them by Your Holy Spirit, so that they will not wallow in self-pity but trust You and speak Your promises over their life in faith.

Father, cover them with a garment of praise. Anoint them with the oil of joy. Let Your joy abide in their heart and change their countenance. Father, help them to watch over their heart with all diligence, for from it flow the issues of life. In Jesus' name. Amen!

Prayer During Times of Adversity

FATHER, I THANK YOU THAT I HAVE VICTORY through Jesus Christ, my Lord. I declare You're my Sustainer and my Strength through these trying times. I am not surprised or shocked at the painful troubles that have come in order to test me as if something strange or unusual is happening to me. Instead, I rejoice that I can share Christ's sufferings, so I may be overwhelmed with joy when His glory is revealed.

I rejoice that, even though for a short time, if necessary, I suffer grief in various trials, so that the genuineness of my faith –more valuable than gold, which perishes though refined by fire – may result in praise, glory, and honor at the revelation of Jesus Christ. I take solace in the fact that, after I have suffered a little while, the God of all grace, who has called me to His eternal glory in Christ, will perfect, establish, strengthen, and settle me.

Father, I shout with a voice of triumph, and I glorify You because this momentary, light affliction is producing for me an eternal weight of glory far beyond all comparison. I will no longer complain, but in everything I give thanks to God, my Father, for this is Your will concerning me.

Prayer of Thanksgiving

THANK YOU, LORD:

for the times You have said "no". They have helped us depend on You so much more.

for unanswered prayer. It reminds us that You know what's best for us, even when our finite minds don't understand.

for the things You have withheld from us. You have protected us from unseen dangers, things that would've ensnared us and people who wanted to destroy us.

for the doors You have closed. They have prevented us from entering seasons, relationships, and places You'd rather not us go.

for the pain, trials and sufferings You've allowed in our lives. How else would we know You as a Healer, Deliverer, Restorer, or a Way-Maker?

for the "alone" times in our lives. When everyone else turned their backs on us, You showed us that You're truly a very present help in times of trouble.

for the uncertainties we've experienced. They have caused us to really rely on You, Your strength, and Your provision, when all our natural, human resources were dried up.

for the times You came through for us when we didn't even know we needed to be rescued. When we couldn't even see the ravenous wolves or the cunning tricks, ditches, snares, and deception of the enemy.

for the losses we have experienced. They have been a reminder that You will restore all that was lost or stolen, all that the cankerworm, the palmerworm, the caterpillar and locusts have devoured.

for the tears we have shed. They are a constant reminder that even though we sow in tears, we will soon reap in joy because You are the lifter of our heads.

that we have an inheritance in the heavenly places, something that this world can never steal from us, the good and perfect gifts that only You can give.

for the greatest gift You could ever give us, the gift of salvation. We could never purchase such a great gift. We say thank You for giving us Your best.

for the righteousness You credited toward us, through the death and resurrection of Jesus. It's a righteousness we could never earn or attain on our own.

that You know us, You hear us, and You see our tears. Remind us through difficult times that You are God and You are on the throne, You are El Shaddai – the all-powerful, self-sufficient, almighty God.

not only for our eternal salvation, but for the salvation You give every day of our lives, as You save us continuously from ourselves, our foolishness, our own limited insights, and our frailties.

Prayer of Thanksgiving and Blessings

WE WILL BLESS THE LORD AT ALL TIMES, and His praises will continually be in our mouths. Our souls make their boast in the Lord. The humble will hear it and be glad (Psalm 34:1). We give thanks in every circumstance, for this is the will of God for us in Christ Jesus (1 Thess 5:18).

...for the Lord our God has turned our mourning into dancing. You have removed our sackcloth and clothed us with joy (Psalm 30:11).

...You've given us beauty for ashes, the oil of joy for mourning, the garment of praise for the spirit of heaviness; so, we will be called trees of righteousness (Isaiah 61:3).

...planted by the rivers of water that brings forth its fruit in its proper season. Our leaves will not wither and whatever we do we will prosper (Psalm 1:3).

...our roots reach deep by the stream, and we will not fear when heat or drought comes. Our leaves will remain green, and we will not be anxious or worried in a year of drought nor will we stop bearing fruit (Jeremiah 17:8).

For Your word says, "the righteous man will flourish like the palm tree and grow strong like the cedars of Lebanon" (Psalm 92:12).

Thank You, Lord, for blessing us and enlarging our territory (1 Chronic. 4:10).

Thank You for bringing us into a good land, a land of brooks of water, fountains and springs flowing from the valley and hills. A land of wheat and barley, vines, fig trees, pomegranates, olive oil, milk and honey. A land where we will eat food without scarcity, and we will lack nothing (Deut. 8:7-9; Ex. 3:8).

Prayer of Thanksgiving
(Let Not Your Heart be Troubled)

HEAVENLY FATHER, WE PRAISE YOU FOR THE GIFT of another beautiful day, for Your mercies are new every morning. We thank You this day for being Jehovah Shalom, our peace. Father, we bind our minds to Your mind, and we declare we have the mind of Christ. We will think on Your goodness and all that You've already done for us. We will think on those things that are true, honest, just, pure, lovely, things of good report and worthy of praise.

We will not be anxious about anything; rather, we lift prayers and petitions to You, with thanksgiving and make every request known to You. And we thank You for Your peace that transcends all our understanding and guards our hearts and minds through Christ Jesus.

Father, please forgive us for trying to handle things in our own way. Free us from the desire to control every situation ourselves. This day, we cast *all* our cares upon You because You care for us. We give You our children, marriages, relationships, dreams, hurts, pains, and disappointments and all our concerns.

Through whatever challenges we face today, we trust in You, Lord, with all our hearts, having the confidence to lean not on our own understanding but, in all our ways, acknowledge You, for You will direct our path.

Today, Father, we are releasing it *all*! We release *all* doubt, anxiety, fear, disappointments, anger, and frustration. We command Your peace to envelop us, so that we can smile and rejoice in the storm. Give us strength to face our battles and emerge victorious through Jesus Christ, our Lord. Father, we trust You, and, as we keep our minds fixed on You, we thank You for a continuous flow of Your perfect peace (inward peace, outward peace, peace with God, peace of conscience, peace at all times, in all events). In Jesus' name, amen.

Prayer Over Finances

HEAVENLY FATHER, WE THANK YOU FOR THIS DAY.
Today we come before You to pray over our finances. Lord, we
bind Satan, all principalities, powers, rulers of the darkness,
wicked spirits in high places, the spirit of poverty and python,
and all spirits not of the Holy Spirit manifesting against our
finances. We loose ourselves and our finances. In the name of
Jesus Christ, we command Satan to release his grip from our
finances. Release our finances, our income, and our possessions
this day and every day to come in the name of Jesus.

Father, we break every spirit of poverty that was inherited
through our bloodlines by the blood of Jesus. We bind all family
curses of poverty and break every satanic chain of poverty off
our lives. In the name of Jesus, we renounce and reverse every
financial curse through the blood of eternal covenants. We
bind and destroy the activities of every evil force that comes
against our harvest and season of reaping, in the name of
Jesus. Every device of the enemy to reroute our wealth through
sickness, sudden death, accidents and financial emergencies, be
destroyed by the fire of the Holy Spirit, in the name of Jesus.

Father, we command Satan to restore a seven-fold return of
all he has stolen from us, for the Word declares, "...when a thief
is found, he must restore all he has stolen seven-fold". Lord,
we know Your word is true and will not return to You void.
We command every leaking pocket, purse, and wallet to be

sealed now, in the name of Jesus. We pull down every financial roadblock and command all crooked places to be made straight. We command all our financial miracles to manifest now! We command all our financial deserts and wildernesses to be turned into springs of water. We bind every work of unfruitfulness in our lives, and we command all barren grounds to be healed, in the name of Jesus.

We trust in faith and call our finances restored, prosperous, and full of God's abundance according to the Lord Jesus Christ's plan for our lives. We are blessed because we walk not in the counsel of the ungodly, nor stand with sinners, nor sit with the scornful. We choose to spend our days delighting in the law of the Lord and meditating on His Word day and night. And because of this, we are like trees planted by the rivers of water that bring forth fruit in our season. And whatever we speak, by Christ, will be. Nothing will be withered, and whatever we do will prosper. We thank You, Lord, for supplying our every need according to Your riches in glory by Christ Jesus. We praise You and glorify Your name for all that You are doing in our lives. We thank You, O Lord, and we magnify Your holy name!

We declare today that we are the seed of Abraham. Your Word declares that You will never leave us or forsake us. We believe this to be true in all aspects of our lives, including our finances. We pray that You would give us a financial strategy to live debt-free and to financially owe no man or woman anything, except to love them. We pray that You would lead us to use strategies that are based on Kingdom principles and developed for Kingdom purposes. Father, help us to correct any financial mistakes that we've made. We repent for being careless stewards of Your finances. We give control of every financial area of our lives back to You. We purpose this day to listen to the Holy Spirit concerning what to do with our finances, the finances You've given to us. Lord, help us to hear Your voice, so that we will make wise financial decisions. Help us to show that You can trust us with more money, and that we'll use them to bring glory and honor to You.

Lord, re-establish Your covenant of prosperity with us. Give us a generous heart and let us give generously to others with a spirit of joy. Help us to sow for the Kingdom of God, looking towards what is to come instead of focusing on the temporary things of the present. We declare it to be so, not by power or might but by the Spirit of the Living God. We thank You that:

> Deuteronomy 5:33 says to "stay on the path the Lord, your God, has commanded you to follow, then you will live long and prosperous lives in the land you are about to enter and occupy".
>
> Psalm 128:2 says that we will "enjoy the fruit of [our] labor", "be happy", and that "it will go well with us" because we fear You.
>
> Proverbs 10:22 says, "The blessing of the Lord makes us rich, and He adds no sorrow with it".
>
> Psalm 112:3 says, "Wealth and riches will continually be in our house and our righteousness will endure forever".
>
> Proverbs 3:9-10 says that, because we honor the Lord with our wealth and the first fruits of our increase, our "barns will be filled with plenty" and "vats will overflow with new wine".
>
> Matthew 6:33 says, "Seek above all else the kingdom of God and His righteousness, and everything we need and want will be given to us".

We thank You for blessing us. We see the wealth raining down on us now. We thank You, Jesus, that You're opening doors of blessings for us, and You're shutting the door of poverty.

Luke 6:38 says that, if we give, we will receive, "good measure, pressed down, shaken together and running over that men will give to your bosom". Philippians 4:19 says, "My God will supply all of our needs according to His riches in glory in Christ Jesus".

We thank You for preparing a table for us in the presence of our enemies. You anoint our heads with oil, and our cups are overflowing with blessings. We thank You that our children are blessed, as well as our spouses, our churches, our neighborhood, community, our state, this country and other nations.

Thank You for turning our situations around doing great and marvelous things in our lives. Christ died so we could live and have wealth and prosperity. We thank You that Your Word says that, if we diligently obey Your voice and carefully observe Your commandments:

You will *set us high above* all nations of the earth
all Your blessings *will come upon us* and overtake us
we will be blessed in the *city*, in the *field*, and in the *country*.
You will bless:
the *fruit* of our body,
the *produce* of our ground,
the *increase* of our herds and cattle and *offspring* of our flocks,
our *basket* and our *kneading bowl*, and
us when we come in and go out
You will cause:

- our enemies to rise against us but be *destroyed*,
- enemies to come against us one way but flee in *seven* different directions.
- a *blessing* to come upon us and our storehouses, so that whatever we set our hands to do will prosper
- us to be established as a *holy people*. If we hearken to the voice of the Lord, all people of the earth will know that we are called by His name, and they will be afraid of us, and the Lord will grant us plenty of goods.

We declare we have access to the double portion of prosperity because we are Abraham's seed and of Jesus Christ. We lack no good thing. The Lord will open heaven and release the rain to our land in its season, and He will bless all the works of our hands. We will lend to many nations, but we will borrow from none. The Lord will make us the head and not the tail. We will be above only and not beneath. We will not turn aside from them to the left or to the right or go after other gods. We will not attempt to gain wealth by any means of the world's system or in an unjust manner. We rebuke and bind the spirit of mammon that tries to convince us to trust in riches and not our heavenly Father. Matthew 6:24 tells us that we cannot serve God and mammon because "either we'll hate one and love the other or hold on to one and despise the other". We sever with the blood of Jesus, the evil root of the love of money that will attempt to spring forth in our lives. When mammon says to "buy and keep", we'll follow Your commandment that says, "sow, and you'll reap". When mammon says to "cheat and steal", we'll obey Your Word and "give and receive".

In the name of Jesus, we bind pride, greed and poverty, saying:

The spirit of *poverty* will not make us ashamed of the blessings of God.

The spirit of *pride* will not have effect in our lives; we will acknowledge God for His wonderful blessings and bountiful harvest.

The spirit of *greed* will not cause us to be covetous, stingy, or sow sparingly yet seek for more.

Father, we command every mountain of lack to be removed from our path, in the name of Jesus. Let every devourer assigned to our finances be destroyed. Let the windows of heaven be opened to us and divine showers of blessings flow on us, in the name of Jesus. By divine appointment, let us come face-to-face with those You've raised up and commanded to bless us.

Father, let us find favor in Your sight and in the sight of all men. Whatever we have lost to the enemy, we take it back by force. We put a stop to it now! Every lack in our lives, be consumed now by the fire of God. By our God, who is overwhelming us with blessings, may every power manipulating our finances be disarmed and deactivated, in the name of Jesus. For as long as heaven and earth endure, seedtime and harvest will remain. So, let every seed we have sown bring forth its assigned harvest, in the name of Jesus.

Father, let the wealth of the wicked be transferred into our hands now, in the name of Jesus. Let rivers flow in our barren heights and springs in our valleys. Let the gate of prosperity be opened. As we go in, we repossess our possessions and finances. We thank You this day for enlarging our territory and for giving us treasures in dark places. We command the riches that are stored in secret places to come to us now! We will never lack anything else. We'll never struggle again financially, and we receive it by faith for us, our children, and our children's children. Our entire bloodline is financially blessed, in the name of Jesus, as we submit our lives to God. We honor You with our lives and with everything that's within us.

Lord, we declare that You are adding *super* to our *natural* and *extra* to our *ordinary*.

We declare no more common blessings or struggle, lack, want, and living from check-to-check, but instead claim ridiculous, outrageous, unexplainable blessings.

We are a royal priesthood and a king's kids. We will no longer live as peasants.

Concerning our finances, the old has gone, and the new has come.

We declare the promises of God over our finances. They are spirit and life; they will not return void or without accomplishing what God sent them to do in their entirety.

Thank You, Lord, for Your ministering angels that grab every word and go before us into this day, week, month, and year, creating divine appointments, connections, and relationships.

You are the God of breakthrough, and we're breaking out of every net of financial difficulty, out of every web of debt, and out of the clutches of the spirit of poverty, old mindsets, and old habits.

We declare it all broken, in the name of Jesus, and we expect a move of God *suddenly* in our finances from this day forth.

We declare that our seeds will not fall by the wayside. Our harvest will not be downtrodden by the enemy or devoured by evil spirits or spirits of poverty. They will not fall on stony ground. Our harvest will spring forth in its proper season. It will not wither or fail to bear fruit. It will not be snuffed out by greed, covetousness or unjust gain. It cannot and will not fall on thorny ground. Our harvest will not be choked out by the enemy or negative confessions we've spoken. It will no longer be hindered, delayed, or in limbo due to worry, doubt, or unbelief.

We command our harvest to come forth and be released now, in the name of Jesus. We declare by faith that our seed will be planted into good ground. Our harvest will come forth in good measure, pressed down, shaken together, and running over. It will yield a hundred-fold return, in the name of Jesus, because it was sown into fertile soil, with the right attitude and a cheerful heart.

Prayer for Financial Breakthrough

FATHER, ACCORDING TO YOUR WORD, WE STAND in unshakable faith, based on Your Word and ready to receive from You. We are tithers and givers. Thank You for providing exceedingly and abundantly above all that we could ask or think. Thank You that You meet all our needs according to Your riches in glory by Christ Jesus and for multiplying our seed sown so that we may give into every good work.

Father, Your Word says that he who supplies seed to the sower and bread for food will supply and multiply your seed for sowing and increase the harvest of your righteousness (2 Cor 9:10). In Jesus' name, we receive now by faith the hundred-fold return on every seed that has left our hands and been sown in fertile ground. Lord, please forgive us for sowing into ground that was infertile, barren, and unproductive. We pray that You would speak to us and direct us on when and where to sow. And because we are willing and obedient to You, we declare we will eat the good of the land. Thank You, Father, for bringing us into "a good land, a spacious land flowing with milk and honey; a land of brooks of water, of fountains and springs; a land of wheat and barley, vines and fig trees and pomegranates and of olive oil; a land where we will eat without scarcity and will lack nothing" (Deu 8:7-9).

Father, we recognize that every good and perfect gift comes from You. Lord, we thank You for all that You've done and all that You're going to do. Father, we ask that You place Your hand on our finances. Father, Your Word says that You have given us the power and ability to get wealth. Lord, bless the works of our hands. We will eat the fruit of our hands, be happy, and it will be well with us (Ps. 128:2).

Your word declares, "Lazy hands make for poverty, but diligent hands bring wealth" (Pr. 10:4). We bind every lazy, slothful, and sluggish spirit, in the name of Jesus. For the soul of the sluggard craves and gets nothing, but the soul of the diligent is made fat (Pr. 13:4). We rebuke and bind the spirit of poverty along with its effects, and we loose the spirit of life, prosperity, overflow, and abundance over our lives.

Lord, You are Jehovah Jireh, and we trust in You to provide every need and to destroy every season of lack. Your Word declares that You hear and answer the prayers of Your people. King David wrote that he had never seen the righteous forsaken or his seed begging for bread (Ps. 37:25). Proverbs 10:3 says, "The Lord will not allow the righteous to hunger". Your Word tells us in Matthew 6 not to worry about our lives, what we will eat or drink, our bodies, or clothing. The birds of the air don't sow or reap, but our heavenly Father feeds them. Are we not more important than they? You told us that our minds should not be preoccupied with these things but should seek first Your kingdom and Your righteousness, and the food, clothing, shelter, and all other things we desire and need will be given to us. We stand on these promises and trust wholeheartedly in Your ability to provide.

Father, we acknowledge and repent of any sins we have committed which would cause our finances to be stifled:

1. Cain—Father, we present every gift or seed with the right attitude. Your Word says You love a cheerful giver, and we give You our very best gift – not what's left over, but we put Yours to the side off top. Before we pay any bills or purchase anything, we vow to give You what's due to You.

2. Malachi—Father, many are cursed because they do not honor You with their tithes and offerings. You commanded us to bring the *whole* tithe into the storehouse, so there may be meat in Your house. You told us to test You in this matter, and You would:
   - open the windows of heaven
   - pour out a blessing so that there will be not enough room to receive it
   - rebuke the devourer for our sake, so that he could not destroy the fruit of our ground
   - not allow our vine to cast her fruit before its time
   - make sure all nations call us blessed
   - see to it that we will be a delightsome land (Mal. 3:10-12)

3. Haggai—Father, we have neglected the care of Your house and Your kingdom, while we are living in luxurious homes. You told us to consider our ways:
   - We have planted much but harvested little.
   - We eat but never have enough.
   - We drink but never have our fill.
   - We put on clothes but cannot keep warm.
   - We earn wages just to put them in a bag with holes.
   - We expect much, but it comes to little or nothing.
   - We bring it home, and You blow it away because Your

house lies in ruin, lack, and want while each man is busy building his own home.

- It's because of our actions that the heavens have withheld the dew and the earth has withheld its produce. Lord, You called for a drought on the land, on the mountains, on the grain, on the new wine, on the oil, on the crops, on the men, on the cattle, and all the labor of our hands.

Father, we repent, and we put Your house first. We will fully obey Your Word and carefully follow Your commandments. You said in Deuteronomy 28 that, if we obeyed You, You would:

- set us high above all other nations on the earth
- allow blessings to come upon us and overtake us
- make sure we would be blessed in the city and in the field
- bless:
  the fruit of our body
  the fruit of our ground
  the fruit of our cattle
  the increase of our herd
  the flock of our sheep
  our basket and kneading bowl (store)
- make sure we would be blessed coming in and going out
- cause our enemies that revolt against us to be defeated before us. They will come against us one way and flee before us seven ways
- command a blessing upon our barns and in all we put our hands to. You will bless us in the land the Lord God gives us.
- establish us as a holy people, if we keep the commandments of the Lord our God and walk in Your ways. So, all the people of the earth will see that we are

called by the name of the Lord, and they will be afraid.

- make us plenteous in goods, in the fruit of our body, in the offspring of our livestock and in the produce of our ground, in the land the Lord promised to our forefathers.
- open Your good treasure, the heavens, to give rain to our land in its season and to bless all the work of our hand.
- make sure we would lend to many nations, but we will borrow from none.
- make sure we would be the head and not the tail; above only and not beneath, if we hearken to the commandments of the Lord, to observe and do them. Do not turn aside from any of the words, to the right or to the left, to go after other gods and serve them.

Lord, where there is doubt, we ask that You help our unbelief. Teach us to remember Your exceedingly great works, Your kindness, and the benefits You've given us. Your Word declares, "Blessed be the Lord, who daily loads us with benefits" (Ps. 68:19). Father, remind us to lean not on our own understanding or that which is in front of us but fully trust in Your sovereignty.

Jeremiah 17:7-8 says, "Blessed is the man who trusts in the Lord. For he will be like a tree planted by the water, that spreads its roots by the river, and will not fear when the heat comes; but its leaves will be green, and it will not be anxious in a year of drought nor cease to yield fruit". God, in this season, as we wait patiently on Your financial provision, we pray that You will renew our strength, so that we'll mount up with wings as eagles, we'll run and not be weary, and we'll walk and not faint (Isa. 40:31). We will not grow weary in doing what is right regarding tithing and sowing seeds, for in due season we will reap the manifold blessings of God if we do not faint (Gal. 6:9).

We release old mindsets, habits and behavioral patterns that have created lack and poverty. We forbid thoughts of failure, defeat, and mediocrity to dwell in our minds. We confess that wealth and riches are continually in our homes and our righteousness will endure forever (Ps. 112:3). Proverbs 14:23 says that in all labor there is profit, so, as we work hard, we command profit margins and surplus to increase. We declare that we will continue to give cheerfully to the Kingdom of God because we know that as we do this, You will generously provide for us and we will always have everything we need and have plenty left over to share with others. We command promotions and financial increase to manifest into our now!

Holy Spirit, rescue those who are drowning in financial debt and help us all to manage our finances better. We bind the spirit of debt and declare financial freedom, in the name of Jesus. We pray we owe no many anything, but the continuing debt to love him (Rom. 13:8). As we receive increases in our finances, help us to remember that abundance comes from You. Please help us to not hoard Your blessings. Your Word says that when we help the poor, we are lending to You and You will repay us for our good deeds (Pro. 19:17). Help us to look for opportunities to be a financial blessing to someone else. Your Word says, "The liberal soul will be made fat, and- he who waters others will be watered (Pro. 11:25). Father, please surround us with Your favor like a shield and continue to open doors of opportunity. Thank You for financial provision, in Jesus' name. Amen.

Finance and Favor Declaration

WEALTH AND RICHES WILL BE IN OUR HOUSES, and our righteousness will endure forever (Ps 112:3).

We have favor with God and with man (Luke 2:52).

We will be satisfied with favor and full of the blessings of the Lord (Deut 33:23).

Father, cause showers to come down in their season; they will be showers of blessings. Cause the trees of the field to yield her fruit and the earth to produce her increase (Ez 34:26,27).

Let Your blessings make us rich and add no sorrow with it (Prov 10:22).

Lord, You load us daily with benefits (Ps 68:19).

Lord, we declare our set time of favor is now! (Ps 102:13)

Let Your favor be upon our lives like a cloud of the latter rain (Prov 16:15).

Surround us with favor like a shield (Ps 5:12).

Let the blessings of Abraham be upon our life (Gal 3:13-14).

Lord, bless our substance and the works of our hands (Deut 33:11).

Cause us to reap a hundred-fold return like Isaac did in the time of famine (Gen 26:12).

Let Your goodness be as the morning cloud and the early dew (Hosea 6:4).

We will not lack any good thing because our God, withhold no good thing from us because we walk upright (Ps 34:8; 84:11).

Thank You Father, for satisfying our mouths with good things; so that Your youth is renewed like the Eagles (Ps 103:5).

"Financially Loaded" Declaration

I speak it into the atmosphere: I'm *loaded* financially. Every need is met. People are looking to give into my life today.

The favor of God is upon me! It goes before me into this day, week, month, and year, creating divine appointments, connections, and relationships for me and opening doors of opportunities *no* man can shut!

I declare that I will experience so many of God's blessings this year that I won't be able to contain them. I believe I receive *overflow*! I'm decreeing and demanding it because I am destined for it. My overflow will be so big, it will cancel out all the losses of the past *and* present.

The favor of God is on me! Therefore, my life will better from this day forward. In Jesus' name, amen and hallelujah!

Prayer for Wisdom

GREAT AND AWESOME GOD, WE HONOR YOU THIS DAY. We continually offer up a sacrifice of praise to You; that is the fruit of our lips that give thanks to Your name. If we had ten thousand tongues, we could not praise You enough. Oh, Lord, my God, You've performed many wonders for us. Your plans for us are too numerous to list. You have no equal. If we tried to recount all Your wonderful deeds, they would be too numerous to count (Psalm 40:5).

James 1:5 says, "If any of you lacks wisdom, let him ask of God, who gives to all generously and without reproach, and it will be given to him". We ask for understanding hearts to judge Your people and to discern between good and evil (1 Kings 3:9). Spirit of the Lord, rest upon us and grant us the spirit of wisdom and understanding, the spirit of counsel and might, the spirit of knowledge and fear of the Lord (Isa 11:2).

Grant us wisdom from heaven that is pure, peaceable, gentle, reasonable, full of mercy and good fruits, impartial and sincere (James 3:17).

Your Word says, "If we ask, it will be given to us; if we seek, we'll find; if we knock, the door will be opened for us (Luke 11:9).

Father, we seek out wisdom, for the words of the wise are gracious, like honey, and much more than gold and silver (Pro 16:16,24:14; Ecc 10:12). Lord, instruct us in the way of wisdom and lead us along a straight path, for those who find it will have a future, and hope will not be cut off (Pro 4:11; 24:14).

We declare by faith that wisdom, understanding, and discretion are our portion, in the name of Jesus Christ, our Lord and Savior.

Prayer for Perseverance

FATHER, WE ARE TRULY LIVING IN THE LAST DAYS, and perilous times are have come. We're experiencing many things in this day and time that try to steal our peace, hope, and faith. Help us, Father, to have full assurance of hope until the end, so that we do not become sluggish but *imitators* of those who, through faith and patience, inherit Your promises (Heb 6:11-12). Help us, Father, not to grow weary in our well-doing, for, in due time, we will reap a bountiful harvest if we don't faint, grow tired, or get weary (Gal 6:9). Lord, strengthen us with all power according to Your glory, so that we may have great endurance and patience and give joyful thanks to You, who have qualified us to share in the inheritance of Your holy people in the kingdom of light (Col 1:11-12).

This day, we lay aside every weight and the sin that so easily entangles us, and we run with endurance the race that is set before us. We fix our eyes on Jesus, the author and finisher of our faith (Heb 12:1-2). In these last days, we will remain steadfast, immovable, and always abounding in the work of the Lord (1 Cor 15:58).

We will pursue righteousness, godliness, faith, love, patience and meekness. We will continue to fight the good fight of faith. We will finish the race and keep the faith, in Jesus' name (1 Tim 6:11-12; 2 Tim 4:7).

Prayer for Running the Race in Purity and Bearing Spiritual Fruit

LORD, WE THANK YOU FOR BEING OUR WONDERFUL COUNSELOR and Guide. We confess that, without You, we can do nothing. We know that, on our own, we will ultimately fail, but, with You, victory is promised. We lay aside every weight and the sin that so easily entangles us, and we run with patience the race that is set before us (Heb 12:1).

We run in such a way to get the prize. We do not run aimlessly or fight like boxers beating the air. We discipline our bodies and bring them into subjection, so, after preaching to others, we ourselves are not castaways or disqualified (1 Cor 9:24-37). We are no longer slaves to sin, which leads to death, but to obedience, which leads to righteousness (Rom 6:16). We cast off the works of darkness and put on the armor of light (Rom 13:12). For we know the unrighteous will not inherit the Kingdom of God, neither fornicators, idolaters, adulterers, effeminates, self-abusers with mankind, thieves, coveters, drunkards, slanderers, or extortioners (1 Cor 6:10).

We will not be deceived because "God is not mocked. For whatever a man sows, that will he also reap. For he that sows to his flesh will of the flesh will reap corruption, but he that sows to the Spirit will of the Spirit reap life everlasting" (Gal 6:7-8). For the wages of sin is death, but the gift of God is eternal life through Jesus Christ our Lord (Rom 6:23). For through the Spirit we put to death the deeds of the body and declare we will live (Rom 8:13). We were buried with Christ by baptism into death, just as He was raised from the dead by the glory of the Father, we too walk in newness of life. If we have been united with Him in death, we will certainly be united with Him in resurrection (Rom 6:4-5). We will walk in a manner worthy of the Lord, to please Him, bearing fruit in every good work and increasing in the knowledge of God (Col 3:10). We put on hearts of compassion, kindness, gentleness and patience, bearing with one another, and forgiving each other (Col 3:12-13). We flee from youthful lusts and pursue righteousness, faith, love and peace (2 Timothy 2:22).

We pray the fruit of the Spirit will manifest in abundance every day of our lives. Father, give us more love, joy, peace, patience, kindness, goodness, faithfulness and self-control, in the name of Jesus.

Prayer Against Fear and our Enemies

─────

FATHER, WE THANK YOU FOR ALWAYS BEING WITH US and, because You are, we will not fear or be dismayed. Thank You for strengthening us and helping us. Thank You for upholding us in Your righteous right hand (Isa 41:10). We boldly declare that, if God be for us, who can be against us? (Rom 8:31). So, we say to the enemy: devise your strategy, but it will come to naught; propose your plan, but it will not stand, for God is with us (Isa 8:10). The Lord is with us as a mighty warrior. Our persecutors will stumble and not prevail. They will be greatly ashamed (Jer 20:11). We stand confidently on Your Word, which says vengeance belongs to You. You will repay our enemies. Their feet will slip in due time, for their day of calamity is at hand, and their doom will come swiftly (Deu 32:35).

We say the Lord is our light and our salvation – whom shall we fear? The Lord is the strength of our lives; of whom shall we be afraid? When the wicked, even our enemies and foes, come up to eat up our flesh, they will surely fall. If a host should encamp against us, our hearts will not fear. Though war should rise against us, in this will we be confident. For in the time of trouble, the Lord, our God will hide us in His pavilion; in the secret of his tabernacle He will hide us. He will set us upon a rock, and our heads will be lifted up above our enemies around us (Ps 27:1-6).

Father, please keep us as the apple of Your eye; hide us in the shadow of Your wings (Ps 17:8). Hide us in the secret place of Your presence from the conspiracies of man. Keep us secretly in a shelter from the strife of tongues (Ps 31:20). Lord, You are our hiding place. You preserve us from trouble. You surround us with songs of deliverance (Ps 32:7). We dwell in the secret place of the Most High, and we abide under the shadow of the Almighty (Ps 91:1).

We say fear has no part in our lives; for You have not given us a spirit of fear but of power, love and of a sound mind (2 Tim 1:7). We rebuke and bind the spirit of fear, and we loose the perfect love of Christ to drive you out. There is no fear in love. The one who fears has not been perfected in love (2 Tim 1:7). We fearlessly confess, we have been perfected in the love of Christ.

Prayer for a New Heart

LORD, WE RETURN TO YOU WITH ALL OF OUR HEARTS, with fasting, weeping and mourning. We rend our hearts and not our garments. We return to You Lord, for You are gracious and compassionate, slow to anger, abounding in loving-kindness and relenting of evil (Joel 2:12-13). We come before You with humble hearts; for You resist the proud but give grace to the humble (James 4:6). The sacrifices of God are a broken spirit: a broken spirit and a contrite heart You will not despise (Ps 51:17).

Father, create in us a clean heart and renew a right spirit in us (Ps 51:0). Remove from us this heart of stone and give us a heart of flesh (Ez 36:26). This day, we rid ourselves of all the offenses we have committed (Ez 18:31). Give us an undivided heart. Give us a heart to know You, Lord (Ez 11:19). From this day forward, we will be Your people and You will be our God (Jer 24:7). Father, put Your law in our minds and write it upon our hearts (Jer 31:33).

Prayer for Circumcising our Heart and Leading Us

LORD, CIRCUMCISE OUR HEARTS AND THE HEARTS OF OUR descendants, so we may love You with all our hearts and soul and live (Deut. 30:6).

Give us a heart to know You, Lord, and then we will be Your people and You will be our God; for we return to You with our whole hearts (Jer. 24:7).

Father, put Your laws in our minds and write them on the tablets of our hearts (Hebrew 8:10).

Keep us from wandering from Your commandments. We have hidden Your word in our hearts that we might not sin against You (Psalm 119:10-11).

We declare our feet will not slip, for the steps of a good man are ordered by the Lord, and He delights in our way (Psalm 37:23-31).

Your word says, "You will protect and ground the feet of the saints". Father, bring us out of the horrible pit and out of the miry clay; set our feet upon a rock and establish our goings (1 Sam 2:9; Psalm 40:2).

With Your help we can run through a troop; with our God we can leap over walls. (Psalm 18:29)

Lord, make our feet like the feet of a deer; and cause us to stand securely on our high places. Teach our hands to war and our fingers to fight, so that our arms can bend a bow of bronze (Psalm 18:33-34).

Through You, the Lord our God, we will do mighty things and gain the victory; for it is He that will trample down our enemies (Psalm 60:12).

They will be as ashes under the sole of our feet on the day the Lord of Hosts has prepared (Malachi 4:3).

We will consume them and wound them until they are unable to rise (2 Sam. 22:39).

...for the enemy we see today, we will never see you again (Exodus 14:13).

We need not to fight this battle. We take our positions and see the salvation of the Lord on our behalf. We are not afraid, discouraged or dismayed; for the Lord is with us (2 Chron 20:17).

The weapons of our warfare are not carnal, worldly or fleshly; but mighty through God to the pulling down of strongholds. We overthrow arguments and cast down imaginations and every high thing that exalts itself against the knowledge of God, and we take every thought captive to make it obedient to Christ (2 Cor. 10:4-5).

We put on the whole armor of God, so we will be able to stand firm against all strategies, tactics and wiles of the devil. So that when the day of evil comes, we will be able to stand our ground, and having done all, to stand firm (Eph. 6:11-13).

We put on the belt of truth. It's buckled around our waist and the breastplate of righteousness is intact; our feet are ready with the preparation of the gospel of peace. We take up the shield of faith to quench every fiery dart of the enemy. And we put on the helmet of salvation. We have in our hands, the sword of the spirit, which is the word of God. We pray in the spirit at all times, with all prayer and petitions; remaining alert and persistent in prayer (Eph. 6:14-18).

We will continue in prayer, being watchful and thankful (Colossians 4:2).

...being sober-minded and vigilant; because our adversary the devil, prowls around like a roaring lion, seeking whom he may devour. We resist him, and we stand firm in our faith knowing our brothers and sisters in Christ are experiencing the same afflictions throughout the world. We understand that after we have suffered a while, the God of all Grace, will perfect, confirm, strengthen, and establish us (1 Peter 5:8-10).

So, Father, we count it all joy when we've fallen into diverse temptation, and we know that the trying of our faith produces patience, and we let patience have its perfect work so that we will be perfect, complete, and not lacking anything (James 1:2-4).

Father, strengthen now the minds of Your people and encourage us to continue in the faith; for we must endure many hardships and afflictions to enter the kingdom of God (Acts 14:22).

Father, in You we have peace and take courage that You have already overcome the world on our behalf (John 16:33).

We say what Your word says about us – that in all things we are more than conquerors through Him that loved us (Romans 8:37).

Thanks be unto God our Father, who gives us victory through our Lord Jesus Christ (1 Cor. 15:57).

We declare, we have been crucified with Christ, and it's no longer us who live, but Christ lives in us. And the life that we live now in the flesh, we live by faith in the Son of God, who loved us and gave Himself for us (Galatians 2:20).

Since we have been united with Him in his death, we will also be raised to life as he was. Knowing that our old man was crucified with him, in order that our body of sin might be done away with, so that we would no longer be slaves to sin (Romans 6:6).

We repent and turn to You, God, so that our sins may be wiped away, in order that times of refreshing may come from the presence of the Lord (Acts 3:19-20).

So, we ask Father, that You would have mercy upon us; according to Your loving-kindness; according to the greatness of Your tender mercies blot out our transgressions. Wash us thoroughly from our iniquity and cleanse us from our sins. Purge us with hyssop, and we will be clean. Wash us, and we will be whiter than snow (Psalm 51:1-2-7).

...though our sins are as scarlet, they will be as white as snow. Though they are red like crimson, they will be like wool (Isaiah 1:18).

Thank You, Lord, for blotting out our transgressions for Your own sake and for removing them as far as the East is from the West (Isaiah 43:25; Psalm 103:12).

Father, create in us a clean heart and renew a right Spirit within us (Psalm 51:10).

Take away the stony heart and give us our heart of flesh (Ezekiel.36:26).

We declare that we are transformed by the renewing of our minds today; so, we can prove what God's good, acceptable and perfect will is (Romans 12:2).

We put on the new man, which in the likeness of God, and has been created in righteousness and Holiness (Ephesians 4:24).

...and we make no provision for the flesh to fulfill its lustful desires (Romans 13:14).

The works of the flesh are obvious: adultery, fornication, uncleanness, idolatry, witchcraft, hatred, strife, jealousy, outbursts of anger, disputes, divisions, envy, drunkenness, orgies, and the like (Galatians 5:19-21).

But as the elect of God we close ourselves with hearts of compassion, kindness, humility, gentleness and patience (Colossians 3:12).

And the fruit of the spirit: love, joy, peace, long-suffering, gentleness, goodness, Faith, meekness, and Temperance are operating in abundance in our lives (Galatians 5:22-23).

We declare the spirit of the Lord rest upon us. The spirit of wisdom and understanding, the spirit of counsel and might, the spirit of knowledge and the fear of the Lord (Isaiah 11:2).

We're increasing and wisdom and statue, and in favor with God and man (Luke 2:52).

Lord, surround us with Your favor as a shield (Psalm 5:12).

Prayer for Favor and Wisdom

LORD, BLESS MY HANDS AND CAUSE EVERY WORK TO PROSPER. Cause me to be skillful in every branch of wisdom and gifted with understanding and discerning knowledge. Bring me into the favor and compassion of my superiors, coworkers, and those who I encounter daily in order to open doors of opportunity. Cause me to stand out among my peers and to be found ten times better than the rest. Lord, gift me with understanding all kinds of dreams and visions.

Lord, wisdom and might belong to You. You change the times and seasons. You remove kings and set up kings. You give wisdom to the wise and knowledge to those who have no understanding. You reveal the deep and secret things. You know what's in darkness, and light dwells with You (Dan 2:21-22).

Prayer for Peace

FATHER, WE THANK YOU FOR BEING JEHOVAH SHALOM, the God of our Peace. Thank You for the spiritual fruit of peace You have given to us (Gal 5:22). It transcends all our understanding and guard our hearts and minds in Christ Jesus (Phil 4:7). We reject all anxiety, worry, frustration, doubt, uncertainty, and anguish. We will not be anxious about anything, but in every situation, by prayer and petition, with thanksgiving, we present every request to God (Phil 4:6).

We will not worry about everyday life–whether we have enough food and drink, or enough clothes to wear. Life is more than food and our bodies more than clothing (Matt 6:25). We will not worry about tomorrow, for tomorrow will worry about itself (Matt 6:34). We cast all our cares on the Lord for He cares for us (1 Pet 5:7). We know that in this world we will have trouble, but we take heart and are encouraged because our Father has already overcome the world (John 16:33).

We thank You, Lord of Peace, for giving us peace at all times and in every way (2 Thess 3:16). Peace not as the world gives; therefore, our hearts will not be troubled or afraid (John 14:27).

We declare peace to everyone far and near (Isa 57:19). It will extend to all like a river (Isa 66:12). We thank You for keeping us in perfect peace because we trust You and keep our minds fixed on You and Your goodness (Isa 26:3). We thank You, Father, for being our Prince of Peace (Isa 9:6).

Prayer for Mercy

FATHER, WE BLESS YOU BECAUSE YOU ARE GRACIOUS, full of compassion, slow to anger and of great mercy. You are good to all and Your tender mercies are over all Your works (Ps 145:8-10). Daily we sin and fall short of the glory of God, but You, Lord, are good and always ready to forgive. You're abundant in mercy to all who call upon You (Rom 3:23; Ps 86:5). Remember not the sins of our youth, our transgressions or rebellious acts (Ps 25:7). Have mercy on us, O God, according to Your loving-kindness; according to Your great compassion, blot out our transgressions (Ps 51:1). Thank You for not always accusing us or harboring anger forever. You haven't dealt with us according to our sins or rewarded us according to our iniquities. For as heaven is high above the earth, so great is Your mercy toward us because we fear You (Ps 103:9-11). Lord, we thank You for Your overflowing mercy.

Prayer for Redemption through the Blood and Salvation

⟨⟩

FATHER, WE THANK YOU THAT CHRIST WAS ONCE OFFERED to bear the sins of many. He will appear a second time, not to bear sin, but to bring salvation to those who eagerly await Him (Heb 9:28). He poured out His life unto death and was numbered with the transgressors; for he bore the sin of many and made intercession for the transgressors (Isa 53:12). He made Himself of no reputation and took on the form of a servant; and being found in appearance as a man, he humbled himself and became obedient to death, even the death of the cross (Phil 2:8). He has saved us and called us with a holy calling; not according to our works but according to his own purpose and grace, that He gave to us in Christ Jesus before the world began (2 Tim 1:9).

Lord, we thank You for saving us be the washing of regeneration and renewing of the Holy Ghost (Titus 3:5). For Your Word says, "unless one is born of water and Spirit he cannot enter into the kingdom of God. That which is born of the flesh is flesh, and that which is born of the Spirit is spirit (John 3:5-6). We know that nothing good lives in us, that is, in our flesh; for we have the desire to do what is good, but we cannot carry it out (Rom 7:14). Father, sanctify us. Cleanse us by the washing with water through the word (Eph 5:26).

Lord, we confess with our mouths "Jesus is Lord," and we believe in our hearts that God raised Him from the dead. It is with our hearts we believe in righteousness and, with our mouths, confession is made to salvation, and we are saved (Rom 10:9-10). We believe that, since we are now in Christ, we are new creatures. All old things are passed away, and all things have become new (2 Cor 5:17). We take off the old man that is corrupted by its deceitful lust and declare that we are renewed in the spirit of our minds. We put on the new man, created to be like God in righteousness and true holiness (Eph 4:22-24). By faith, we confess we are redeemed by the Blood of the Lamb and are new in Christ.

Prayer to Become a Living Sacrifice in Humility and Love

FATHER, WE PRESENT OURSELVES A LIVING SACRIFICE – HOLY, acceptable to God, which is our reasonable service. Help us not to be conformed to this old world but to be transformed by the renewing of our minds that we may prove what the good, acceptable, and perfect will of God is (Rom 12:1-2). Help us to live a life worthy of the calling we have received, with all lowliness and meekness, with longsuffering, forbearing one another in love (Eph 4:1-2). Help us to please You and to be fruitful in every good work and increasing in the knowledge of God (Col 1:10).

Lord, help us to be devoted one to another in brotherly love; doing nothing out of selfish ambition or vainglory; but in humility consider others more important than ourselves. Help us to not look out for our own personal interests but also for the interests of others (Rom 12:10; Phil 2:3-4). We who are strong in our faith, will bear the infirmities of the weak and not to please ourselves (Rom 15:1). Even if our brother or sister be overtaken in a fault, we who are spiritual, will restore them in a spirit of meekness; being watchful of ourselves, or we may fall into the same temptation. So, we will bear one another's burdens and fulfill the law of Christ. For if a man think himself to be something, when he is nothing, he deceived himself (Gal

6:1-3).

We cannot and will not take the pleasure of looking down on our brothers and sisters, for we all have sinned and come short of the glory of God (Rom 3:23). So, we will love our neighbors as ourselves (Mark 12:31). For if anyone claims to be in the light but hates his own brother/sister, he is still in darkness. He that loves his brother abides in the light, and there is nothing in him to make him stumble. But he that hates his brother is in darkness and walks in darkness and knows not where he goes because that darkness has blinded his eyes (1 John 2:9-11). Father, help us to love like You.

Prayer for Spiritual Cleansing

FATHER, WE DRAW NEAR WITH SINCERE HEARTS, in full assurance of faith, having our hearts sprinkled clean from evil consciences and our bodies washed with pure water (Heb 10:22). We ask that You baptize us – not the removal of dirt from the flesh, but a plea to God for a good conscience (1 Pet 3:21). We bow down and cry out to You as the leper in Matthew 8:2. We say, "Lord, if You are willing, You can make us clean". We come and reason with You. Though our sins are as scarlet, they will be white as snow. Though they are red like crimson, they will be like wool (Isa 1:18). Father, purge us with hyssop, and we will be clean. Wash us, and we'll be whiter than snow (Ps 51:7). Cause Your fountain to be opened and cleanse us from sin and uncleanness (Zec 13:1). We declare boldly by faith, we are sanctified and justified by the Blood of the Lamb.

Prayer of Breakthrough

I DEMAND BREAKTHROUGH THIS DAY! I will not leave the presence of God without it manifesting in my life. Father, You said in Your word that we have not because we haven't asked anything of You (James 4:2). We ask today for Your power. We ask for Your anointing to destroy every yoke!

Today is not a regular day!

I declare today is the day of our turn-around. It is the day of our deliverance, salvation, and breakthrough!

I declare, as Jacob did, "[I] will not let You go until You bless [me]" (Gen 32:26).

Fill my cup, Lord, to the overflow!

I empty myself.

I declare with boldness: less of me and more of You!

I will not leave Your presence the same way I came.

I demand breakthrough in my body, spirit, mind, finances, marriage, relationships, etc.

I declare *breakthrough*.

Prayer for Our Nations (Global)

LORD, YOU ARE GREAT. YOU KEEP YOUR COVENANT of mercy to those who love You and obey Your commandments. We have sinned and have committed iniquity. We have departed from Your laws. We have not listened to Your prophets who spoke in Your name. You have allowed our enemies to rise over us. Nations and terrorists from the ends of the earth have come to threaten us because of our sins. Lord, according to Your righteousness, let Your anger and fury be turned away. Hear the prayers of Your people and cause Your face to shine upon us. Your word declares that Your anger is but for a moment, but Your favor is for a lifetime. You're a compassionate and gracious God, slow to anger and abounding in mercy. You will not always accuse us, nor will You remain angry forever. You do not treat us as our sins deserve or repay us according to our iniquities. It is because of Your mercies we are not consumed; for Your compassions never fail.

We have become a reproach to all nations that surround us. We will no longer call evil good and good evil. We will have nothing to do with fruitless deeds of darkness but rather expose them. Lord, open our eyes so that we'll turn from darkness to light, from the power of Satan to God, that we may receive forgiveness of sins and an inheritance among those who have been sanctified by faith. Lord, we repent this day because the kingdom of heaven is at hand. Lord, blot out our sins, so that times of refreshing can come in Your presence. Lord, we don't hide our shortcomings, but we confess them and turn away, so we can find mercy.

The signs of the end times are upon us, and the day of our Lord is at hand. Your Word declares that we will know of Your coming by these signs:

- Nation rising against nation
- Kingdom rising against kingdom
- Pestilence, famine, and earthquakes in various places
- Wars and rumors of wars
- Many killed for their faith
- Deception abounding and the love of many growing cold
- Distress of nations upon the land
- False Christs and false prophets rising, displaying signs and wonders, possibly deceiving the very elect

Perilous times have come upon us and are prevalent.
2 Timothy 3:1 says many will be:

lovers of themselves,

covetous (lovers of money),

boasters (boastful),

proud (arrogant),

blasphemers (verbally abusive),

disobedient to parents,

unthankful (ungrateful),

unholy (*"These men have certainly crept into the churches and as a result the churches are full of unconverted, unholy people today, who have turned the grace of God into a license to sin!"* -Jude 1:4).

without natural affection (unloving), (1 Corinthians 6:9-10

says, "...Do you not know that the unrighteous will not inherit the kingdom of God? Do not be deceived. Neither fornicators, nor idolaters, nor adulterers, **nor homosexuals**, nor sodomites, nor thieves, nor covetous, nor drunkards, nor revilers, nor extortioners will inherit the kingdom of God")

    truce-breakers (unforgiving),
    false accusers (slanderous),
    incontinent (without self-control),
    fierce (brutal),
    despisers of those that are good (haters of good),
    traitors (betrayers),
    heady (reckless),
    high-minded (conceited),
    lovers of pleasures more than lovers of God,
    having a form of godliness, but denying the power of God

Many are being deceived by the prince of the power of the air, and he is craftily using the tools at his disposal – mainly, communication: television, radio, the internet, Facebook and other social media outlets – in order to convince people to accept the anti-Christ and damnation.

We recognize and expose the subtlety of the serpent and how deception is plaguing our households. Lord, send us as laborers in this end time harvest to preach and declare the acceptable year of our Lord, to proclaim deliverance to the captives, the recovery of sight to the blind, to set at liberty those that are oppressed and bruised. We declare it to be so, not by might or by power but by the Spirit of the Living God. Anoint us. Fill us with Your Spirit in these last days, amid all the worldliness, the lust of the flesh, the lust of the eye, and the pride of life. Holy Spirit do a mighty work. Help us to be aware of the hour we are living in so that You can use us to carry out great exploits.

We pray for the nation, government and our leaders. You told us that supplications, prayers, intercessions, and thanksgiving, are to be made for all men; for kings, presidents, and for all that are in authority; that we may lead a quiet and peaceable life in all godliness and honesty. We plead the blood of Jesus over every position that has been appointed or elected. We pray for our president, vice president, all the Cabinet, the chief justices of the Supreme Court and all those in authority, that You would give them Your wisdom and discernment as they lead. Protect the president and his family from terrorist attacks and assassination. We pray for the members of the Senate and the House of Representatives to find Your peace and direction, and for these men and women to act and lead according to Your Word.

A house divided against itself cannot stand, so we pray for them to be unified in righteousness for the sake of the nation. Father, make their hearts and ears attentive to godly counsel, doing what is right in Your sight. We pray for Your protection to cover all law enforcement officers and men/women of the military. We pray that they do not usurp their authority, but they protect and serve the citizens of our land. We pray over the minds of the people that they will be separated from the puppet strings of the prince of the power of the air. We sever all cords that would cause principalities, powers, rulers of the darkness of this world, and spiritual wickedness in high places to control the offices of our generation. Lord, deliver us from the oppression of the ungodly in high places. Your word declares when the righteous are in authority, the people rejoice, but when the wicked bear rule, the people mourn. Lord, give us leader like:

The king of Nineveh—when he heard the warning of Jonah, he stepped down from his throne and humbled himself. He took off his royal robes and covered himself with sackcloth and sat down in ashes. He issued a decree that no one, including animals from the herds and flock were to eat or drink anything. Everyone was to pray earnestly to God and turn from their evil ways and from violence.

Cyrus the Great—leaders that are sensitive to the plans and purposes of God. God raised him up to release the Israelites from Babylonian captivity.

King David—a man after God's heart. He had a deep desire to follow God's will and do "everything" God wanted him to do. He loved God's word and diligently hearkened to His commandments.

King Solomon—will rule with wisdom, discernment and authority

King Josiah—Judah's greatest King. He loved God's law and encouraged the people to trust God. He instructed them to rebuild the house of God.

Remove the scepter of authority from leaders like:

King Saul—who usurped his authority. He took the people's sons and forced them to become servants. He took their daughters and their land. He taxed the people, by taking a tenth of their money to pay his servants.

King Pharaoh—who was arrogant and raised up to display the glory of God. He said, "Who is the Lord that I should obey his voice to let Israel go? I know not the Lord, neither will I let Israel go." The Lord said, "For this cause have I raised you up, to show you My power and that My name is to be declared throughout all the earth.

King Nebuchadnezzar—prideful, arrogant, a tool of correction against God's people. God dethroned him and took his glory. He was driven from man and his heart became that as an animal. After he was humbled by God for seven (7) years, he lifted his eyes and his understanding and kingdom was returned.

Father, remove the veils and scales of idolatry from our eyes.

Let all leaders given to idolatry, sexual perversion and illegal activity be delivered expediently or exposed and dealt with. Let every undercover agenda, conspiracy, dark covenant, satanic network, racist spirit, and antichrist spirit in any of our political leadership be cursed to the root, in Jesus' name. Let every agenda set to hinder, water down, cause compromise, and send persecution against those who preach the unadulterated gospel of Jesus Christ be judged. Let every veil of deception spread over America be destroyed. As deception is removed, allow laws to be passed where our children will be taught of the Lord, and our nation be filled with the glory of the Lord. We sprinkle America with the blood of Jesus and pray that the leaders of the nation will be under that covering. Let all plans of terrorism against our country, our leadership, and our people be dried up at the root, never to manifest in Jesus' name.

We declare our Redeemer is strong. The Lord of Hosts is His name. He will vigorously plead our case so that He may bring rest to the earth, but turmoil to every enemy. Our witness is in heaven, and our Advocate is on high. We know our Redeemer lives, and that at last He will take His stand on the earth. The enemy is waging war against the saints, and it seems as if he's prevailing (overpowering, defeating) us, but the Ancient of Days will come to pronounce favor on the saints of God, and we will possess the kingdom. For the God of peace will soon crush Satan under our feet. We bruise the head of the enemy and declare that he's a defeated foe. We overcome the enemy by the blood of the Lamb and by the words of our testimony. Lord, let Your kingdom come and Your will be done on earth as it is in heaven. For Your kingdom is an everlasting kingdom, and Your dominion endures throughout all generations. For the Lord God is the King of all the earth and sits on the throne forever. He rules by His power forever. He watches over the nations; from His dwelling place He looks out on all inhabitants of the earth. Nothing in all creation is hidden from His sight. Everything is uncovered and laid bare before Him. For the eyes of the Lord are in every place, watching the good and the evil; defending the poor and fatherless; bringing justice to the afflicted and needy. He treats the poor fairly and make right decisions for the downtrodden of the earth. He will strike the earth with the rod of His mouth, and the breath of His lips will slay the wicked. Righteousness will be the belt around His loins and faithfulness the belt around His waist. He brings princes and rulers to nothing. He makes the judges of the earth useless. They hardly get started or take root, and He will blow on them and they will wither. The whirlwind will carry them away as stubble. The Lord bring the counsel of the heathens to nothing. He makes the devices and plans of the people of non-effect. Both the counsel of the Lord stands forever, and the thoughts of his heart to all generations. Blessed is the nation whose God is the Lord, the people whom He has chosen from His own inheritance.

God, You, founded this nation and we see it going straight to hell at a fast pace. It has gone over the morality cliff. We pray that the eyes of the people be opened across the land in:

Brazil	Dominican Republic	Greece
Australia	Britain	United Kingdom
South Africa	North and South Korea	Venezuela
Japan	France	Egypt
India	Europe	Turkey
Israel	Saudi Arabia	Canada
Iraq	Lebanon	Jordan
Haiti	Singapore	China
Russia	Pakistan	Asia and Kuwait

Lord, we've strayed so far from You. We've become very secular and the laws and regulations go against Your Word. We come before You, in the name of Jesus Christ, the only begotten Son, praying for an outpouring of Your Holy Spirit upon our nation. Bring revival to every city, town and every part of our country, and to every church. We pray there not be any dead churches or ministries, but they be filled with new life in You. We pray for unity in the body of Christ and bridge denominational gaps. Help us to proclaim the gospel as revealed in Your Holy Word so that the eyes of the blind be opened to see who You really are. Bring multitudes into Your Kingdom through faith in Jesus Christ. Let this revival be so powerful that it affects every part of our nation and every part of the world. We ask that You raise up Christian leaders and pastors who would not compromise their integrity and the Holy Word of God and who will resist temptation to be immoral or disobedient to Your statutes. Give them revelation so they will have the perfect word at the right time. Give them a powerful voice to speak into the lives of many, especially in times of tragedy or national concern when their ears and minds are most opened to hear You. Help them to point people in the right direction so that new life and the standard of morality will be higher than it has been. Enable these leaders and ministers to lead people into a closer relationship with the Living God, and this country will again become a God-fearing nation. We confess that we have been a rebellious people who have doubted You and made light of Your word. Forgive us for shutting You out of our lives. We confess as the body of Christ, that we have not always maintained a consistent commitment in prayer. Our prayers have been powerless because we have not always lived or prayed Your way. Remove the blinders from our eyes where we are deceived. Help us to move out of darkness and into Your marvelous light so we can be Your light extended to others. Teach us how not to be overcome by evil but overcome evil with good.

Father, we pray that You would remove the veil of doubt that has blinded the mind of people that do not know You. We know that if the gospel is veiled, it is veiled to those that are perishing, whose minds the god of this age has blinded; who do not believe unless the light of the gospel, the glory of Christ who is the image of God, should shine on them. We know that if people could really see You for who You are, they would see the light and not reject You. Reveal Yourself to them. Open their eyes so they may see Your wondrous works. For those who know the scriptures but don't know You, reveal Jesus, the Living Word, and make Your Word come alive to them. We pray for many to receive Jesus as their personal Lord and Savior. We pray for our neighbors, family members, our spouses, children, friends, our mayors, congressman, governors and the President of this country. We ask that You reveal Yourself to every one of them. Send believers into their lives to tell them about You in a way that opens their eyes to Your goodness. Bring them into the full knowledge of You, Jesus our Savior. Father, You said that whoever calls on the name of the Lord will be saved. We pray that men and women everywhere will call on Your name and be saved.

Father, Your word says where there is no revelation, the people cast off restraint but happy is he who keeps the law. Father, we pray for a revelation of Yourself to people that they will love Your law and reject anything that is not Your way. Set us free from people who will try to keep us from talking and teaching about You. Deliver all who have a form of godliness but deny Your power. On the behalf of our nation we repent for pornography, racism, prostitution, abortion, robbery, greed, idolatry, murder, sexual sins, lust, covetousness, adultery, faithlessness and all injustices. Have mercy on our nation for the abominations in the land. Father, deliver us from the consequences of every one of them, and convict the hearts of all who participate in these things. Bring us to our knees before You right now. Let this nation remember from where we have fallen, repenting and returning to doing our first work, setting our hearts and souls to seek You, Lord; humbling ourselves, praying and turning from our wicked ways. Then, You would hear us, forgive our sins and heal our land.

Father, we know Your heart is moved with compassion for Your people who are weary and scattered like sheep having no shepherd, and You are not willing that any man should perish but that all come to repentance. Lord, raise up a standard in our nation. Cause the rains of Your Spirit to flood our land and revive Your works in the midst of us. Raise up intercessors for our nation to pull down strongholds over this land. Remind us as Your people, to pray always with all prayer and supplication in the Spirit and being watchful to the end with all perseverance and supplication for all the saints. Help us to open our mouths and speak boldly about the wonders of Your mighty Word, Your love, grace, truth and Your soon return, in the name of Jesus Christ.

Prayer for our Government

FATHER, WE COVER THE ***LEGISLATIVE BRANCH***. Bring order now to the Senate and House of Representatives. Father, as laws are written, discussed and voted on let them be made based on the foundation of Your Word and not on popular opinion.

Place the righteous in the position of Senators and House of Representatives and cause their voices to be heard above all others. Lord, give them wisdom to make sound judgments as they rule in the place of authority You've given them. Your Word says, "A house divided against itself cannot stand"; therefore, I pray for them to be unified in righteousness for the sake of the nation.

Father, we call the ***executive branch*** to be in divine order of Your will. Touch now the President of the United States as he approves and carries out laws passed. Give him wisdom as he negotiates bills and treaties and acts as head of state and commander in chief for the armed forces. Lord, as the Vice President and other cabinet members come together to make decision for our government, we pray they will consult You above all. Father, give them direction. Your Word says, "Where there is no guidance, the people fall, but victory is won through many advisers". We know that every governing authority has been established by You. So, Father, give them what they need to make better decisions for the welfare of Your people. Father, give godly counsel to every cabinet member who advises the President on important matters, and let them not fall on deaf ears. Turn the counsel of every conspirator to foolishness, as You did to Ahithophel. Remove their influence and frustrate the plans of the crafty so that their hands cannot accomplish what they had planned!

Lord, we declare that justice will once again be seen in our *judicial branch* as it oversees the court system of this country. Father, righteousness and justice are the foundation of Your throne, and we pray for our President and Senators who have the responsibility of placing judges in our courts to use their authority in ways to advance justice. We pray they select capable men from all the people—men who fear God, trustworthy men and women who hate dishonest gain.

Please protect this process from all obstruction and send us men and women of wisdom, who respect Your law. Father, give us a Chief Justice and Associate Justices with humility, who seek Your truth and not their own opinions. We pray this nation be once again founded on the oracles of Your Word, and that we once again become one nation, under God, indivisible, with liberty and justice for all; regardless of gender, race, color, creed, nationality and religious background. We pray that justice roll down like water and righteousness like a mighty stream. Father, many of our sons and daughters' blood cry out to You from the ground due to police brutality and those who usurp their authority. Lord, vindicate the weak and fatherless; Do justice to the afflicted and destitute. Rescue the weak and needy; Deliver them out of the hand of the wicked.

We call for the mourning, wailing women to come quickly and cry for us, until our own eyes are flooded with tears. For death has come up into our windows; it has entered our homes, cutting off the children and young men from the streets. Dead bodies lie like dung on the open field, like cut grain behind the reaper, with no one to gather them.

2 Chronicles 7:14 says, "if my people, who are called by my name, will humble themselves and pray and seek my face and turn from their wicked ways, then I will hear from heaven, and I will forgive their sin and will heal their land." Father, we seek Your face on today and ask that You hear our earnest cry. Have mercy on us as we repent of every wicked way. Forgive our sins, Lord, and release Your healing virtue upon America and all adjoining nations.

We pray for Israel, Your chosen people, Your treasured possession. Lord, You promised Abraham in Genesis 12:2-3, "I will make you into a great nation and I will bless you; I will make your name great, and you will be a blessing. I will bless those who bless you, and whoever curses you I will curse; and all peoples on earth will be blessed through you. Many think that You've deserted Your people, but Isaiah 49:15-16 says, "Can a mother forget the baby at her breast and have no compassion on the child she has borne? Though she may forget, I will not forget you! See, I have engraved you on the palms of my hands. For a brief moment I forsook you, but with great compassion I will gather you. In a little anger I hid My face from you for a moment, but with everlasting loving-kindness I will have mercy on you, says the LORD your Redeemer". No longer will they call you Forsaken or your land Desolate; for I, the Lord, take delight in you and claim you as My Bride. Many may ask, "Has God rejected His people? Absolutely not! By no means! Did they stumble and fall beyond recovery? Of course not! But by their transgression salvation has come to the Gentiles, to make Israel jealous." (Is. 54:7-8; 62:4; Rom. 11:1-11).

Father, You made an everlasting covenant between Abraham, Isaac, and Jacob, as well as their descendants. Despite their rebellion, Lord, You promised You would never break Your covenant with them or alter Your own agreement (Judges 2:1; Ps. 89:34). We are assured today that God is not a man, that he should lie, or a son of man, that He might change his mind. Does He speak and not act, or promise and not fulfill? Even when we are faithless, He remains faithful, for He cannot deny Himself (Num 23:19; 2 Tim. 2:13).

We lift every U.S ambassador to Israel. Father, give them wise communications and supportive relationships with their Israeli counterparts. We pray for Israeli Prime Minister and President. May You give them continued strength and resolve for their people. Father, bestow upon them supernatural wisdom as they lead and a heart desire for You. Give them a boldness to lead this nation in perilous times.

We pray for the protection of the Jewish people and Israel. There are numerous groups and organizations who are bent on their destruction, and they want to annihilate this nation. Father, send military aid for physical protection of this nation, its people, its defenses, and its land. Confuse the language and relationships of Iran, Venezuela and Islamic terrorist groups that join in their endeavors against Your people. We cover their land with the Blood of Jesus, and we declare a "No Fly Zone"! There will be no nuclear weapons, suicide bombings, kidnappings, car bombings, rocket launches against Your people. We pray for the peace of Jerusalem. May they prosper who love You. May peace be within Your walls, and prosperity within Your palaces. For my brothers and companions' sake I will say, "Peace be within you! "For the sake of the house of the LORD our God, I will seek your good. (Ps. 122:6-9)

Prayer for Protection for the First Family of the United States

FATHER, WE PRAY FOR THE PRESIDENT AND HIS FAMILY. Please protect them from the evil that is in the world and keep them safe and free from all harm, hurt, and hidden dangers. Father, we praise You that they dwell in the secret place of the Most High and that they shall remain stable and fixed under the shadow of the Almighty—whose power NO foe can withstand. We solely depend on You God to be their refuge and fortress.

We declare the first family is delivered from the snare of the fowler and from the deadly pestilence. You have covered them with Your feathers, and under Your wings will they trust and find refuge. Lord, we pray that You will give peace and sustain them and make them dwell in safety. The Trumps will not be afraid of the terror of the night, nor of the arrow (the evil plots and slanders of the wicked) that flies by day, nor of the pestilence that stalks in darkness, nor of the destruction and sudden death that surprise and lay waste at noonday. A thousand may fall at their side, and ten thousand at their right hand, but it shall not come near them. *No weapon formed against them will prosper!* In Jesus' name, Amen.

Prayer for our Nations (U.S.)

YOUR WORD SAYS, "I SOUGHT FOR SOMEONE that would make up the hedge and stand in the gap before me for the land, that I should not destroy it: but I found none" (Ez. 22:30). Lord, we stand continuously in the gap for our nation. We stand on our post as watchmen on the walls; praying day and night, continually. We take no rest or keep silent, but continually remind You of Your word (Isa. 62:6). LORD, we confess our wickedness and the iniquity of our ancestors. We have sinned against You. For Your name sake, do not despise us; do not dishonor Your glorious throne. Remember Your covenant with us and do not break it (Jer 14:20-21).

Romans 13:1 – Let everyone be subject to the governing authorities, for there is no authority except that which God has established. The authorities that exist have been established by God.

Jeremiah 29:7 – Also, seek the peace and prosperity of the city to which I have carried You into exile. Pray to the LORD for it, because if it prospers, you too will prosper.

II Chronicles 7:14 – if my people, who are called by my name, will humble themselves and pray and seek my face and turn from their wicked ways, then I will hear from heaven, and I will forgive their sin and will heal their land.

Psalms 2:10-11 – Therefore, you kings (presidents), be wise; be warned, you rulers of the earth. Serve the LORD with fear and celebrate his rule with trembling.

Proverbs 11:14 – Where there is no guidance, the people fall, but victory is won through many advisers.

Proverbs 21:1 – The king's heart is a stream of water in the hand of the LORD; he turns it wherever he will.

Job 12:23 – He makes nations great, and destroys them; he enlarges nations, and scatters them.

Proverbs 2:1-8 – My son, if you accept My words and store up My commands within you, turning your ear to wisdom and applying your heart to understanding— indeed, if you cry out for knowledge and understanding, and if you look for it as for silver and search for it as for hidden treasure, then you will understand the fear of the LORD and find the knowledge of God. For the LORD gives wisdom; from his mouth come knowledge and understanding. He stores up sound wisdom for the righteous; he is a shield to those who walk upright, for He guards the course of the just and protects the way of His saints.

Prayer to the Lord, Our Savior and Deliverer

THE EYES OF THE LORD ARE ON THOSE WHO FEAR HIM, on those who hope in his loving-kindness, to deliver their soul from death, and to keep them alive in famine (Psalm 33:18-19).

... for his ears are inclined to their prayer, but the face of the Lord is against those who do evil (1 Peter 3:12).

Our soul waits for the Lord. You are our Help and our Shield (Psalm 33:10).

You are our rock, our fortress, our deliverer, our God, our rock, in whom we take refuge. Our shield and the horn of our salvation, my stronghold (Psalm 18:2).

For who is God besides the Lord? And who is The Rock except our God? (Psalm 18:31)

For our hearts rejoice in You because we trust in His holy name (Psalm 33:21).

Declaration of Who I am in Christ

FATHER, I THANK YOU FOR THIS DAY; a day that wasn't promised to me. I boldly confess this is the day the Lord has made. I will rejoice and be glad in it (Ps 118:24). Today I call on the Lord, He answers, and He shows me great and mighty things that we had no previous knowledge of (Isa 33:3).

Today, I will get a greater revelation of who I am in Christ. I thank You, Lord, that because I have been made the righteousness of God that I have been completely justified by faith apart from the works of the law (2 Cor. 5:21). I praise You, God, because I have peace with You, and that I can stand in Your presence without guilt or without shame.

I declare that I will no longer let Satan deceive me into thinking that I am unworthy. I thank You that because of the Blood of Jesus that I am no longer a slave to sin or living under the curse of the law.

Because of what Jesus has done for me, I have been delivered out of the control and the dominion of darkness, and You have transferred me into the Kingdom of the Son of Your Love. (Col 1:13)

Father, In the Name of Jesus I release Your Word now into the spirit realm to affect the things in the natural realm so that Your purpose for my life will be fulfilled. I declare that no devil in hell will prevail against what You have blessed me with or what You have prepared and prearranged for me. I declare according to Your Word that it all belongs to me. You said all that is Yours is mine, and I declare that I have been given rights here on this earth, and I will exercise those rights by standing on Your Word.

I thank You, Father, that Your eyes are roaming to and fro throughout the whole earth to show Yourself strong on my behalf today (2 Chron. 16:9).

Father, thank You that I am the apple of Your eye and that You have a picture of me in the palms of both Your hands. Today, Lord, because of what You have done for me, I can walk in true freedom that I now live by faith and not by sight.

Thank You, Lord, that I will never have to do anything alone, for You will always be here for me. You promised to never leave me, abandon me, or forsake me. No matter what, thank You, Father, that I have Your promise that nothing can ever separate me from You and Your love and that You will never stop loving me.

I declare today: I am a child of God by faith in Christ Jesus. Amen.

Prayer for Cancer Patients

HEAVENLY FATHER, I PROCLAIM YOUR RIGHTEOUSNESS and praise all the day long. Your faithful love endures forever, and Your mercies never cease. Great is Your faithfulness. Who can compare to You? I exalt Your Holy and Righteous Name. You are the Holy One of Israel who sent Jesus, my Lord and Savior, to redeem all mankind from the curse of the law of sin and death. Thank You for Your healing power. Thank You, Lord, for declaring me as an overcomer by the blood of the Lamb and by the word of my testimony.

Father, Your thoughts towards me are of peace and not evil, to give me a future and a hope. I believe that it is Your will that I live free from all diseases. Lord, I declare that the infirmity of cancer is destroyed, in the name of Jesus! I command every cancerous deformed cell to die at its root and the metastasizing cells to cease from spreading throughout my body, especially to the lungs, bones, liver brain and other organs. I command the increased production of healthy cells to destroy renegade cells. I declare that abnormal cells will die and not enter into my bloodstream or my lymphatic system. Lord, by the power You've given me through Your Son, Jesus, I declare I will not die; but live to tell of Your wondrous works. Lord, I confess that by Your stripes I am healed, redeemed, restored and set free from cancer and its symptoms. I declare the blood of Jesus flows through my veins, permeating my entire being and supernatural healing is flowing throughout my body, in Jesus Name. You are the Lord that heals, and I thank You that You sent Your Word and healed and delivered me from all destruction. Thank You that You bore every one of my griefs and carried my sorrows. Thank You for being wounded for my transgressions and bruised for my iniquities. I declare by Your Word, the chastisement of my peace was upon You and by the thirty-nine stripes You received on Your body, *I am already healed!*

I pray that every medication prescribed by the doctors work effectively to promote health and healing. I rebuke and bind all adverse effects and negative side effects, in the name of Jesus. Father, give the oncologists, physicians, surgeons, and nurses the wisdom, knowledge, and understanding needed to give me the correct prognosis/diagnosis and the skill necessary for my recovery. I disallow and forbid all medical malpractice and errors, in the name of Jesus.

I declare the divine strength of God over my life. Thank You for renewing my strength as the eagles so I can run and not be weary, walk and not faint. Increase my endurance and patience as I undergo x-rays, chemotherapy, radiation therapy, biological therapy, hormone therapy, surgery, cryosurgery and/or other procedures. For Christ's sake, I will delight in weakness, hardships, and difficulties; for when I am weak, Your Spirit will make me strong! Your Word says that you give power to the faint, and to those who have no might You increase strength. Father, increase my strength during this season of testing.

I will not be anxious about any matter, but in everything by prayer and supplication with thanksgiving I will let every request be made known to You, God my Father. And the peace of God will surpass all my understanding, and it will guard my heart and mind. I don't fully understand why You have allowed for me to endure this, but I count it all joy! I know the testing of my faith will produce patience. Patience will have its perfect work, so that I may be perfect, complete and lacking nothing. I declare this light and momentary affliction is producing for me an eternal weight of glory far beyond all comparison!

Lord, You are my Redeemer and Healer. You make all things new. Thank You for my new body and restored health. Your light will break out like the dawn, and my healing will spring up quickly. Lord, forever Your Word is settled in heaven. I have declared Your Word by faith, and it will not return to You empty or void, but it will accomplish and prosper in the purpose it was sent to do. *I am healed*, in Jesus' name, amen.

Prayer for Kawasaki Disease

FATHER, WE COME BOLDLY BEFORE YOUR THRONE to obtain grace to help in time of need. We thank You for the lives of our loved ones, and we come interceding for them now. We plead the blood of Jesus over them, from the crown of their head to the sole of their feet, and we declare that Your name is greater than Kawasaki disease. Your Word says, "[You] bore our griefs and carried our sorrows. Though we considered [You] punished, stricken and afflicted by God; but [You] were wounded for our transgressions, [You] were bruised for our iniquities. The punishment that brought us peace was on [You], and by the thirty-nine lashes [You] received on [Your] body, we are healed now!" (Isaiah 53:4-5).

Father, Your Word says in Jeremiah 30:17, "*You will restore my health and heal my wounds*". By the power of the True and Living God, we command our loved one's body to come into divine alignment to the Word of God and this declaration of faith. We declare there will be:

NO inflammation in their coronary arteries

NO more fever

NO extremely red eyes (conjunctivitis)

NO rash on their body

NO dry, cracked lips or swollen tongue

NO swollen, red hands and feet

NO swollen lymph nodes in their neck or body

NO irritability

NO joint pain

NO diarrhea

NO vomiting

NO abdominal pain

NO acquired heart disease

NO aneurysms

NO heart attacks, and

NO life-threatening internal bleeding

We forbid any malfunctions in their body, in the name of Jesus. We command their immune system to be strengthened to fight off every bacterium. "You sent Your Word and healed them and delivered them from destruction" (Psalm 107:20). The Blood of Jesus flows throughout their veins, permeating healing and wholeness to every organ, tissue, blood cell, nerve, and system in their body. We declare they will live and not die but declare the works of the Lord (Psalm 118:17). Sun of Righteousness, we fear Your name! Arise with healing in Your wing and breathe upon them (Malachi 4:2). Their body will not be deceived by any virus, disease, germ or infection; neither will it work against their life or health in any way. Every cell that does not promote health and healing is cut off from its life source, in the name of Jesus.

Father, give life to their mortal body through Your Holy Spirit (Rom. 8:11). We declare their heart is strong and every beat is normal. It carries the life of God throughout their entire body restoring life and health abundantly. In the name of the Lord Jesus Christ, their arteries will not shrink or become clogged. Their arteries are clean, elastic and function as God created them to function. We declare they have overcome this sickness by the Blood of the Lamb and by the words of this testimony (Rev. 12:11).

Your favor surrounds them, as a shield so we know that no weapon—of disease or infirmity—formed against them will prevail for this is their inheritance as Your child (Psalm 5:12; Is. 54:17). We thank You because what the enemy has hidden in darkness You have exposed and covered with Your precious Blood. We smear the Blood of the Lamb on the doorpost of their room and the death angel cannot penetrate it (Ex. 12:7). Cover every physician, nurse or tech that comes in contact with them. Give them wisdom to give the correct diagnosis, prognosis and medications.

Lord, we have not forgotten all the benefits You've given us. Father, thank You for forgiving our sins, and we thank You for healing them from every disease, for redeeming their life from destruction, for crowing them with lovingkindness and tender mercies; for satisfying their mouth with good things so that their youth is renewed like the eagle's (Psalm 103:1-5).

Father, we have confidence in You, that if we ask anything according to Your will, You hear us. And because You hear us, our petitions and requests will be granted (1 John 5:15). By faith we know Your Word will not and cannot return void. It will accomplish and bring to fruition the very things we have spoken according to Your Word. We declare by faith, they are healed and made whole now! In Jesus' name, Amen.

Prayer for Kidney Recipient

ALMIGHTY GOD, I COME BEFORE YOU with thanksgiving in my heart and a praise on my lips. O Lord, I honor You and revere You because You're so Majestic and Sovereign in all Your ways.

O Lord, I come thanking You now for the life of my loved one. As they have made the journey of what the doctors have diagnosed as kidney failure, You've kept them strong in mind, spirit and body. You've been there all the way. I thank You for being Jehovah Rapha. I thank You now for bringing healing to his body through a kidney transplant. I thank You now for the miracle.

I thank You, Christ, for redeeming them from the curse of the law, having become a curse for them. You bore their every sickness in Your body on the tree, that they might live for righteousness and, by Your stripes, they are already healed. I declare this today, You sent Your word and healed them. They will live and not die and continue to declare the works of You, O' God.

I pray today that every test comes out normal, with no deficiencies. The surgery will go forth with success. Their body will not reject their new kidney. I bind every obstacle, abnormality, and every negative report in the name of Jesus. I declare his kidney will function in the perfection to which God created it to function, and I forbid any malfunction in his body in the name of Jesus. Father, through Your Word, You've imparted life into them. I declare, it's flowing now through their bloodstream. It flows to every cell, tissue and organ, restoring and transforming their health. The Holy Spirit that raised Jesus from the dead dwells in them, permeating His life through their veins, sending healing throughout their body.

O Lord, I plead the blood of Jesus over them from the top of their head to the soles of their feet, over the operating room, over every surgeon, every nurse, every operating device. Guide the surgeon's hand. Keep them alert and attentive. Today, I declare a *positive* report, in the name of Jesus. Cover their mind. I bind anxiety and fear. For You haven't given them a spirit of fear but of love, power and a sound mind. O Lord, give them peace that surpasses all understanding.

I thank You now that all is well and for the victory. In Jesus' name, amen and hallelujah!

Prayer for Kidney Transplant Recipient

DEAR LORD, YOU ARE THE ONE WE TURN TO FOR HELP in moments of weakness and times of need. I ask You to be with Your servant. I thank You Lord for sending out Your Word and healing their body. In the name of Jesus, drive out all infirmity and sickness from their body. I plead the blood of Jesus over their very life. Cover them now from the top of their head to the soles of their feet. I bind any and all malfunctions in the name of Jesus. Their kidney will not reject, and they will function to the perfection which You created them to.

Father, I ask You to turn this weakness into strength, suffering into compassion, sorrow into joy, and pain into comfort for others. May Your servant trust in Your goodness and hope in Your faithfulness, even in the middle of this situation. Let them be filled with patience and joy in Your presence as they wait for Your healing touch and total healing. Oh Lord, bind up every wound; cease all pain and sorrow. Fill them with joy unspeakable. For the joy of the Lord is their strength. Keep their mind. I declare today that fear is far from them, and they shall walk in love, power and a sound mind. Renew their strength as the eagles. Redeem their life from destruction. Satisfy their mouth with good things. Let a praise stir in their heart so that they sing songs of praise and thanksgiving for all the glorious things You've done.

Please restore Your servant to full health, dear Father. Remove all fear and doubt from their heart by the power of Your Holy Spirit, and may You, Lord, be glorified through their life. For they shall live and declare Your works and recount Your wondrous acts. I thank You, Lord, that they prosper in every way and their body may be kept well even as their soul prospers. I thank You, Lord, for this light, momentary affliction is more abundantly preparing and producing an everlasting weight of glory and anointing that outweighs, supersedes, and outlasts it all. I declare today that Your healing power rests upon them now and every person they come in contact with will be comforted and delivered from every spirit of infirmity because Your Spirit rests upon them.

Oh, Lord, we thank You this day for all that You've done and for all that You continue to do. In Jesus' mighty name. Amen.

Prayer against Pneumonia

LORD, I COME BEFORE YOU WITH THANKSGIVING in my heart. I acknowledge You today as the True and Living God. I petition You on today on the behalf of my loved one.

Father, I come thanking You now for their very life. I thank you for being Jehovah Rapha, for You are the Lord who heals. Despite the doctor's diagnosis of pneumonia, I know that Your name supersedes every ailment we will ever encounter. In the name of Jesus, I bind the spirit of infirmity. By the authority and power given to me by Jesus Christ, I command that every germ, bacteria and virus be cut off from its life source. I declare their immune system is strong and the antibiotics are working properly and effectively. I command their lungs to release any and all fluids, in the name of Jesus.

I thank You, Christ, for redeeming them from the curse of the law, having become a curse for them. You bore their every sickness in your body on the tree, that they might live for righteousness and, by Your stripes, they are already healed. I declare this day that You sent Your word and healed them. They shall live and not die and declare Your wondrous works.

Father, through Your Word, you've imparted life into them. I declare that it's flowing now through their bloodstream. It flows to every cell, their lungs, esophagus and throat restoring and transforming their health. O Lord, I plead the blood of Jesus over them from the top of their head to the soles of their feet.

I thank You, Lord, that my petition has been heard, and I praise You in advance for complete healing. In Jesus' name. Amen.

Prayer for Israel

FATHER, WE COME TO YOU IN JESUS' NAME TO PRAY FOR ISRAEL, the Lord's portion, the apple of Your eye, and Your crown of splendor (Zec 2:28; Deu 32:9; Is. 62:3). Psalm 122:6 says we should pray for the peace of Jerusalem. As Your people, we know it's Your will to bless Israel. We ask You, Father, to keep them safe in this time of unrest and turmoil. We thank You, Lord, that no weapon that is formed against Israel will prosper (Isaiah 54:17), for You are protecting them according to Your Word.

You told Abraham in Genesis 12:2-3, "I will make you into a great nation, and I will bless those who bless you, and whoever curses you I will curse; and all peoples on earth will be blessed through you." Father, You are the Rock and Redeemer of Israel. We don't understand the violence and suffering as many are injured and killed, but we pray for justice, Your sovereignty and righteousness to be displayed swiftly. Lord, we pray for mercy for Your people, the governments, military and those in authority. We ask for Your kingdom to come and rule over the land.

Shield the nation of Israel, Lord. Protect the soldiers and civilians from bloodshed. May Your truth and light shine in darkness. We declare Your Word as in Psalm 83, Father, do not keep silent any longer. For Your enemies make an uproar against Your people. Those who hate You have raised their heads. They lay crafty plans against Your people; they consult together against Your treasured ones to wipe out the nation, so their name will be remembered no more. Many nations have risen and conspired against You: the Edomites, Ishmaelites, Moabites, Ammonites, Hivites, Canaanites, Amalekites, Egyptians, and many other nations. Father, make them like whirling dust, like chaff before the wind. As fire consumes the forest, as the flame sets the mountains on fire, so may You pursue them with Your storm and terrify them with Your hurricane! Fill their faces with shame, that they may seek Your name. Let them be put to shame and discouraged forever; let them perish in shame that they may know that You alone, whose name is the Lord, is the Most High over all the earth.

Lord, You said in Your word that You will strike every nation and people that has fought against Jerusalem with a plague. Their flesh will rot while they stand on their feet, their eyes will rot in their sockets, and their tongues will rot in their mouths. On that day a great panic from the Lord will fall on them. They will seize each other and attack one another. The Lord will defend the people of Jerusalem; even so, the weakest among them will be like David, and the house of David will be like God; for the angel of the Lord will go before them. (Zech 14:12, 13; 12:8). Lord, we pray that You would touch the heart of the president of the United States and government officials to come to the aid of Israel. We pray that we will be their ally and not partake in vicious attacks against Your people who You have called by Your name.

Father, Your word says, "For Zion's sake I will not hold my peace, and for Jerusalem's sake I will not rest, until her righteousness goes forth as brightness, and her salvation as a lamp that burns." (Isa. 62:1). Father, You bound Yourself by Your own prophecy, saying that You would only come back and rule in Jerusalem when Israel's leaders ask You to reign as King over them. Jesus grieved in Matthew 23:37, 39 saying, "O

Jerusalem! How often have I wanted to gather your children together, but you were not willing, for I say to you, you will see Me no more until you say, 'Blessed is He who comes in the name of the Lord.'" Father, we ask that You sprinkle clean water on the people of Jerusalem and remove all their filthiness and every idol. Give them a new heart and put a new spirit within them. One that reverence You and longs for You to be their King. Take away their stony heart and give them a heart of flesh. One that is sensitive to Your voice and ready to obey You at all costs. Put Your Spirit in them and cause them to walk in Your statutes and to be careful to keep Your ordinances. Bring them back to the land that You gave their forefathers. You said they will again be Your people and You would be their God." (Ez. 36:25-28). Father, pour out on the house of David and the people of Jerusalem a spirit of grace and supplication, so they will look on You whom they have pierced; and they will mourn for You as one who mourns for an only son. They will weep in bitterness for You, like the bitter weeping over a firstborn. (Zec 12:10). And it shall be that whoever calls on the name of the Lord will be saved and there will be deliverance. (Joel 2:32)

Where there is only hatred, cause Your love to prevail. Bring Your salvation to Israel and draw every heart to You, in the name of Jesus. Amen.

Prayer for Protection

HOLY FATHER, BY THE POWER OF YOUR NAME, we're not asking You to take us from the world, but that You save us from the evil one (John 17:15). Father, be a wall of fire around us (Zec 2:5). Create over our dwelling places a cloud of smoke by day and a flaming fire by night; Your glory will also be a canopy and a defense (Isa 4:5). We boldly confess, we will live in peaceful dwelling places, in secure homes, in undisturbed places of rest (Isa 32:18). Violence will not be heard in our land nor devastation or destruction within our borders; but we will call our walls Salvation and our gates Praise (Isa 60:18).

The Lord is our fortress, our stronghold and our deliverer, our shield, and in Him we take refuge (Ps 144:2). The angel of the Lord camps round about those who fear Him and delivers them (Ps 34:7). We declare, a thousand may fall at our side, and ten thousand at our right hand; but terror, arrows, plagues or calamities will not come near us (Ps 91:6-7). For the name of the Lord is a strong tower; we run in and are safe (Prov 18:10). For the Lord will cover us with His feathers and under His wings we will trust (Ps 91:4). For the Lord has been our defense and refuge in the time of trouble (Ps 59:16).

We say with confidence, we are not afraid of those who have set against us all around; for the Lord is our hiding place and our shield (Ps 3:6; 119:114). You told us to call on You in the day of trouble, and You would deliver us, and we would glorify

You. We call upon Your name, Mighty One, and we thank You for delivering us from the fowler's snare and from the deadly pestilence (Ps 50:15; 91:3). We say the Lord is our keeper. He will preserve our going out and our coming in. The sun will not strike us by day nor the moon by night (Ps 121:5-8). We certainly know that if it had not been for the Lord on our side, our enemies would have overtaken us; the waters would have overwhelmed us, and the stream would have gone over our souls (Ps 124:2-4). But we rest in the fact that our help is in the name of the Lord, who made the heavens and the earth; and as the mountains surround Jerusalem, so He is around His people (Ps 124:8; 125:2).

Father, please continue to deliver us from the evil man and keep us from the violent man. We ask now that You would redeem our lives from destruction and crown us with loving-kindness and tender mercies, in the name of Jesus (Ps 140:1; 103:4). Amen.

Prayer for Protection and Safety

WE DECLARE BY FAITH, THE ANGEL OF LORD CAMPS ROUND ABOUT those who fear Him and delivers them, and because we fear Him, we are delivered from the forces of hell. Though a thousand may fall at our side and ten thousand at our right hand, no pestilence, disease or famine will come near us. The name of Lord is a strong tower; the righteous runs into it and are safe.

Father, we thank You for covering us with Your feathers; under Your wings, we find refuge, in the name of Jesus, for the Lord God has been our Defense and refuge in the day of trouble. We declare, we will not afraid of those who have set against us all around. For You are our hiding-place and our shield. We hope in Your Word.

Lord, You told us to call on You in the day of trouble and You will deliver us. Surely You will deliver us from the fowler's snare and from the deadly pestilence. He who keeps us will not slumber or allow our foot to be moved. Lord, You are our keeper. Preserve our going out and our coming in from this time forth and forevermore. The sun will not strike us by day, nor the moon by night.

We know that if it had not been for the Lord on our side, our enemies would have overtaken us; the waters would have overwhelmed us, the stream would have overwhelmed us, and the fire would've burned us. We rest in the fact that our help is in the name of Lord, who made the heavens and earth. For as the mountains surround Jerusalem, so the Lord surrounds His people from this time and forever.

Father, continue to deliver us from the evildoers and keep us from the plans of the wicked. We ask now that You would continuously redeem our lives from destruction and crown us with loving-kindness and tender mercies. With grateful hearts, we say thank You and declare that it is so, in the name of Jesus, amen.

Prayer for my Mind

I BIND EVERY EVIL SPIRIT THAT'S TRYING TO TORMENT ME! I bind confusion, frustration, restlessness, worry, and depression. I loose God's incomprehensible peace into my life. Jesus, I give You the spirit of heaviness in exchange for the garment of praise (Isa 61:3).

I give thanks in all things, for this is the will of God concerning me in Christ Jesus (1 Thess 5:18). Satan, you are a defeated foe, and I declare that your weapons and schemes are null and void; they will not prosper!! My thoughts are fixed on things that are true, honorable, right, pure, lovely, admirable, excellent and worthy of praise (Phil 4:8).

I have the mind of Christ (1 Cor 2:16[b]). Satan, I give you an eviction notice! You will not inhabit my mind rent free! Every thought and vain imagination that has exalted itself against the knowledge of God is brought into captivity *now* to the obedience of Christ (2 Cor 10:5)! In Jesus' name!

Prayer against Oppression

I STAND IN AGREEMENT THAT THE SPIRIT of oppression, depression and suicide is bound, in the name of Jesus. I declare the peace of God will guard our hearts and minds; the garment of praise covers us and the oil of joy saturates us (Phil 4:7; Isa 61:3).

I declare *no more* heaviness, *no more* mourning, *no more* frustration, *no more* worries, and *no more* anxiety! For the Lord, our God, bore our griefs and carried all our sorrows (Isa 53:4).

I declare our minds are bound to the mind of Christ. We will think on things that are true, honorable, just, pure, lovely, commendable, things of excellence, and anything worthy of praise (Phil 4:8).

We trust You, Lord! We will keep our minds fixed on You and Your goodness, and we're grateful that we're recipients of Your *perfect peace* (Isa 26:3). Amen.

Prayer for Provision and Protection

WE BELIEVE THAT THIS YEAR OF RESTORATION and the years to come will be seven years of plenty. In the name of Jesus, we break down all strongholds keeping us from our blessings. We declare that our mouths will be filled with laughter and our tongues will sing songs of joy, for our God is doing great and mighty things in our lives. Thank You for restoring our prosperity. We declare that all our years of fruitlessness will be transformed into fruitfulness, with a mighty harvest, in the name of Jesus. Thank You for restoring all that the cankerworm, palmerworm, locust, and caterpillars have devoured. We declare that greater is He who dwells in us and nothing is impossible for us.

We decree that, throughout the remainder of this year, our families will dwell in the secret place of the Most High God. We will rest in the shadow of the Almighty, for You are our refuge and our fortress. Thank You for saving us from the fowler's snare and the deadly pestilence. Thank You for covering us with Your feathers. Under Your wings, we find refuge, in the name of Jesus.

Prayer for Spiritual Gifts and Gifts of Grace

FATHER, WE LOVE YOU, AND WE AVAIL OURSELVES TO YOU. We thank You for the various gifts You have given to us through Your Holy Spirit. There are differences in administration, but the same Lord. There are various operations, but it is the same God who operates all of them in all people. To one is given:

the word of wisdom

the word of knowledge

faith

the working of miracles

prophecy

discerning of spirits

various kinds of tongues

the interpretation of tongues

All these works are empowered by the Holy Spirit who gives to each person as he wills (1 Corinthians 12:4-11).

Father, help us to not think we are better than we really are. Help us to be honest in our evaluation of ourselves, measuring ourselves by the faith God has given us. For just as our bodies have many parts and each part has a special function so it is with the body of Christ. We are many parts of one body, and we all belong to each other. We have different gifts according to the grace given to us. If one's gift is prophecy, let him prophesy according to his measure of faith; if serving, let him serve; if teaching, continue to teach. If it is to encourage, then give encouragement; if giving, let him give generously; he who leads, let him lead with diligence; if it is showing mercy, let him do so with cheerfulness (Romans 12:3-8).

God has blessed us with one of His many wonderful gifts to be used to serve others. We will be good stewards and use those gifts well. If any man speaks, let him speak as the oracles of God; if he serves, let him with the ability God gives, so that in all things God may be praised through Jesus Christ. All glory and power to him forever and ever! Amen. (1 Peter 4:10-11)

Prayer for the Fivefold Ministry Gifts and Functions

Father, You've given the gift and function of the apostles, prophets, evangelists, pastors and teachers for the perfecting of the saints, for the work of the ministry, and for the edifying of the body of Christ: until we all reach unity in the faith and in the knowledge of the Son of God and become mature, attaining to the whole measure of the fullness of Christ (Eph 4:11-13). We pray their works will continue until the return of Christ. We cancel the lie of the enemy that says these offices have been done away with. Lord, protect them and keep them as they fulfill their kingdom assignments. Help them so they are not humiliated, confounded or ashamed. Make their faces like flint (Isa 50:7). Be their vindicator. Contend with those that contend against them. Be their strength in trying times. When everyone else is quitting and throwing in the towel, help them to remain steadfast, unmovable and always abounding in the work of the Lord, knowing their labor is not in vain in the Lord (1 Cor 15:58).

Father, we cover each office and function according to Your word. We pray for the *apostles* who are set forth by God to minister with God-given governmental authority to establish churches and lay foundational truth.

May they:

- continue to lay the foundation of the church with solid biblical teaching, and that she comes into full maturity; so, the bride will be presented at the coming of Christ without a spot, wrinkle or blemish (Eph 5:27),
- be granted divine wisdom, knowledge and understanding to train and raise up leaders who will come into full maturity of the gospel, to release them, and plant them where they will reap a great harvest from their labor,
- operate in the gifts of healing, faith, working of miracles, word of wisdom, discerning of spirits, and prophecy,
- be empowered with the Holy Ghost to display signs, wonders and mighty acts.

We thank You for Your *prophets* who You've sent to release a clarion call to Your people and to reveal the heart, mind and will of God. You've set them over nations and kingdoms to root out, to pull down, to destroy, to throw down, to build, and to plant (Jer 1:10). You've made them as a fortified city, a pillar of iron and as walls of bronze against the whole land, kings, princes, priests and to the people of the land (Jer 1:18). May they:

- be used by God in this last day to give direction and correction to the body of Christ;
- edify, exhort, comfort, build up, stir up, encourage and strengthen Your people,
- speak only as the Holy Spirit gives utterance. May they not fill Your people with false hopes or prophesy false visions, divinations, idolatries and the delusions of their own minds. (Jer 23:16; 14:14). May they not add to or subtract from Your message,
- flow freely in the prophetic in areas of guidance, instruction, rebuke, judgment and revelation,

- declare even the hard messages: messages of correction, of impending judgment, or calls of repentance; let them be sealed with mercy and as a result build up and not tear down,
- be granted supernatural ability to recognize God's gifts and callings on individuals and activate those gifts by the laying of the hands.

We cover the *evangelists* who You've designated to proclaim Your good news across the world. May they:
- maintain passion and vision for winning souls to Jesus Christ,
- be sent out as laborers by the Lord of the harvest to gather the end-time harvest,
- be endowed with power to be effective witnesses of Jesus Christ everywhere--Jerusalem, Judea, Samaria, and to the ends of the earth,
- bring the lost to salvation (Acts 1:8),
- preach the gospel with great conviction that will be followed with signs and wonders to confirm their message, and
- be ready at all times to declare the gospel, reprove, rebuke, exhort with patience, be watchful and endure afflictions.

Father, we stand in the gap for all *pastors* who You've commissioned to shepherd local church ministries. May they:
- be given the grace to teach, exhort, protect, correct, comfort and discipline;
- watch over Your sheep, feed Your lambs, and protect them from ravenous wolves in sheep clothing;
- keep watch over our souls as those who will give an account. Let them do this with joy and not with grief (Heb 13:17);

- be loaded with daily provision for every area of ministry. All financial needs are met because all members are 100% tithe payers and seed-sowers.

Lord, we thank You for the *teachers*, for they have been ordained by You to teach and edify the church. May they be given knowledge to explain and interpret the living truths of Your word with simplicity.

Father, we thank You for being head of the body, which is the church. You make the whole body fit together perfectly. As each part does its own special work, it helps the other parts grow, so that the whole body is healthy and growing and full of love (Eph 4:16).

Psalm 91:
Prayer of Protection

I DWELL IN THE SECRET PLACE OF THE MOST HIGH, and I abide under the shadow of the Almighty. I will say of the Lord, "He is my refuge and my fortress, my God; in Him, I will trust". Surely, He will deliver me (my spouse, children, and family) from the snare of the fowler and from the perilous pestilence.

He will cover me (us) with His feathers, and, under His wings, I (we) will trust Him. His truth will be my (our) shield and buckler. I (We) will not be afraid of the terror by night, the arrow that flies by day, the pestilence that walks in darkness, or the destruction that lays waste at noonday.

A thousand may fall at my (our) side, and ten thousand at my (our) right hand; but it will not come near me (us). Only with my (our) eyes will I (we) look and see the reward of the wicked. Because I (we) have made the Lord, who is my (our) refuge, even the Most High, my (our) habitation, no evil will befall me (us), nor will any plague come near my (our) dwelling.

He will give His angels charge over me (us), to keep me (us) in all my (our) ways. They will bear me (us) up in their hands, lest I (we) dash my (our) foot against a stone. I (We) will tread upon the lion and the cobra, the young lion and the serpent I (we) will trample under foot.

Because I (we) have set my (our) love upon Him, He will deliver me (us). He will set me (us) on high because I (we) have known His name. I (We) will call upon Him, and He will answer me (us). He will be with me (us) in trouble; He will deliver me (us) and honor me (us). With long life He will satisfy me (us) and show me (us) His salvation.

Psalm 119-126 Prayer

I AM BLESSED BECAUSE MY WAYS ARE BLAMELESS, and I walk according to the law of the Lord. I am blessed because I keep his statutes and seek him with all my heart. I choose this day to follow the ways of the Lord and to fully obey His precepts and not forsake them. I will be steadfast in following Your decrees; as a result, I will not be put to shame. I will praise You with an upright heart as I learn Your righteous laws. I will stay on the path of purity by living according to Your word. I seek You with all my heart; do not let me stray from Your commands. I have hidden Your word in my heart that I might not sin against You. Praise be to You, O Lord; preserve my life according to Your word. Cause me to understand the way of Your precepts. When my soul is weary with sorrow, strengthen me according to Your word. Keep me from deceitful ways and be gracious to me. Give me understanding, so that I may keep Your law and obey it with all my heart. Turn my heart towards Your statutes and not toward selfish gain. Turn my eyes away from worthless things; fulfill Your promises to me as Your servant, so that I may be feared. O Lord, in Your righteousness preserve my life.

Father, may Your unfailing love and salvation come to me, O Lord, according to Your promises; for I trust in Your Word. Never take Your word of truth from my mouth, for I have put my hope in Your laws. You are my portion, Lord, and I seek

Your face with all my hearts. O Lord, be gracious to me. Lord, I thank You that Your Word is eternal, and it stands firm in the heavens. Your faithfulness continues through all generations and it endures forever. Father, keep my feet from every evil path. I thank You that Your word is a lamp to our feet and a light to my path. You are my refuge and shield. Sustain me according to Your promise and I will live. Do not let my hope be dashed. Uphold me and I will be delivered. Turn to me and have mercy on me, as You always do to those who love Your name. Direct my footsteps according to Your Word; let no sin rule over me. Redeem me from oppression and make Your face shine on me.

I call on You, Lord, in times of distress and know that You'll answer. Save me, Lord, from lying lips and from deceitful tongues. I lift my eyes to the hills, from where my help comes from; for all my help comes from the Lord, who made heaven and earth. I am confident You will not let my foot slip; You, the one who keeps me, will not slumber. You, the one who watches over Israel, will neither slumber nor sleep. The Lord is my keeper. You are the shade on my right hand; the sun will not harm me by day or the moon by night. The Lord will keep me from all harm. He will watch over my very life; the Lord will watch over my coming in and going out from this day forward.

I truly can say, if it had not been for the Lord on my side, my enemies would have swallowed me alive, the flood would've consumed me, swept over me, and swept me away. But praise be to the Lord who hasn't let me be devoured by my enemies. I have escaped the fowler's snare. It has been broken, and I have escaped! I declare this day; my help is in the name of the Lord!

Father, I thank You that You have restored my fortunes, all that has been lost or stolen. My mouth is filled with laughter and my tongue with songs of joy for the great things You've done for me. I declare Your word today, though I sow in tears I will reap in joy! I will recover all today: my finances, my children, my ministry, my peace, my joy and my mind. In the name of Jesus. Amen.

APPENDIX

Evil Spirits and Their Functions

ABANDONMENT
isolation
loneliness
not feeling wanted
not belonging
victim

ADDICTIONS
alcohol
food
gambling
drugs (Rx or non-Rx)
pornography
television
video games

ANGER
hatred
rage
resentment
temper tantrums

ANXIETY
burden
fatigue
heaviness
nervousness
restlessness
weariness

BITTERNESS
blaming
murmuring
critical judging
ridicule
unforgiveness

COMPETITION
jealousy
possessiveness
pride

CONFUSION
indecision
lack of focus
memory lapse
disconnected thoughts
inability to grasp simple truth
ADD, ADHD, OCD

(Taken from The Spiritual Warfare Bible*)*

DECEPTION
confusion
lying
self-deception

DEPRESSION
despondency
despair
discouragement
hopelessness
insomnia
oversleeping
self-pity

suicide
withdrawal

ESCAPE
fantasy
forgetfulness
lethargy
procrastination
withdrawal

GREED
covetousness
idolatry
stealing
fraud

FEAR
anxiety
burdens
heaviness
superstition
phobias: *authorities, failure, punishment, death, infirmities, cancer, heart attack, diabetes, worry*

FINANCIAL PATTERN
compulsive shopping
greed
inability to plan and save
irresponsible spending
poverty

GRIEF
loss
sadness
sorrow
suffering

INFIRMITY/DISEASE
accidents
arthritis
asthma
barrenness
cancer
diabetes
fatigue
heart disease
hypertension
miscarriage
mental illness
migraines
premature death

MENTAL ILLNESS
craziness
compulsions
confusion
hallucinations
hysteria
insanity
paranoid schizophrenia
mental anguish

OCCULTS

astrology
black magic
casting spells or hexes
crystal ball
divination
fraternities or sororities
free masonry
hypnosis
horoscopes
Levitation
necromancy
New Age
Ouija board
palm or psychic reading
voodoo
witchcraft
white magic
yoga

Body Systems and Their Functions

The **circulatory system** is to move blood, nutrients, oxygen, carbon dioxide and hormones around the body. It consists of the heart, blood, blood vessels, arteries and veins.

The **digestive system** consists of a series of connected organs that together, allow the body to break down and absorb food, and remove waste. It includes the mouth, esophagus, stomach, small intestines, large intestines, rectum, and anus. The liver and pancreas also play a role in the digestive system because they produce digestive juices.

The **endocrine system** consists of eight major glands (pineal, pituitary, thyroid, adrenal, pancreas, ovaries, and testes) that secrete hormones into the blood. The hormones, in turn, travel to different tissues and regulate various body functions, such as metabolism, growth and sexual function.

The **immune system** is the body's defense against bacteria, viruses and other harmful. It includes lymph nodes, the spleen, bone marrow, lymphocytes (including B-cells and T-cells), the thymus and leukocytes, which are white blood cells.

The **lymphatic system** includes lymph nodes, left ducts and lymph vessels and plays a role in the body's defenses. Its main job is to make and move lymph, a clear fluid that contains white blood cells, which help the body fight infection. The lymphatic system also moves excess lymph fluid from bodily tissues and returns it to the blood.

The **nervous system** controls both voluntary action (like conscious movement) and involuntary actions (like breathing) and sends signals to different parts of the body. The central nervous system includes the brain and spinal cord. The peripheral nervous system consists of nerves that connect every other part of the body to the central nervous system.

The **muscular system** consists of about 650 muscles that Aid in the movement, blood flow and other bodily functions. There are three types of muscle: skeletal muscle which is connected to Bone and helps with voluntary movement, smooth muscle which is found inside organs and help to move substances through organs, and cardiac muscle which is found in the heart and helps pump blood.

The **reproductive system** allows humans to reproduce. The male reproductive system includes the penis and the testes, which produce sperm. The female reproductive system consists of the vagina, the uterus and the ovaries, which produce eggs. During conception, a sperm cell fuses with an egg cell, which creates a fertilized egg that implants and grows in the uterus.

The **skeletal system**, which contains of 206 bones that are connected by tendons, ligaments and cartilage. The skeleton not only helps us move, but it also involved in the production of blood cells and the storage of calcium. The teeth are also part of the skeletal system, but they aren't considered bones.

The **urinary system** helps eliminate a waste product called urea from the body, which is produced when certain foods are broken down. The whole system includes two kidneys, two ureters, the bladder, to sphincter muscles in the urethra. Urine produced by the kidneys travel down the ureters to the bladder and exit the body through the urethra.

The skin, or **integumentary system**, is the body's largest organ. It protects us from the outside world and is our first defense against bacteria, viruses and other pathogens. Our skin also helps regulate body temperature and eliminate wastes through perspiration. In addition to skin, the integumentary system includes hair and nails.

Organs of the Body

Trachea
Veins
Lungs
Diaphragm
Liver
Gall Bladder
Kidneys
Urethras
Appendix
Bladder
Urethra
Arteries
Heart
Esophagus
Stomach
Spleen
Pancreas
Small Intestines
Large Intestines
Rectum

The Names of God

Abba
Advocate
Advocate
All-Sufficient One
Almighty God
Alpha and Omega
Ancient of Days
Author and Finisher of My Faith
Bread of Life
Bright and Morning Star
Buckler
Chief Cornerstone
Comforter
Consuming Fire
Creator
Deliver
Emmanuel
Everlasting Father
Everlasting God
Everlasting King
Faithful and True
Father
Father
Great Physician
Great Shepherd
Guide
Holy One
Holy Spirit
I Am
King of Glory

King of King
Lamb of God
Lifter of My Head
Light of The World
Lion of Judah
Living Water
Love
Man of War
Master
Mediator
Messiah
Mighty God
My Butler
My Defense
My Deliverer
My Exceeding Joy
My Fortress
My Friend
My Glory
My Help
My Hiding Place
My Hightower
My Redeemer
My Refuge
My Rock
My Savior
My Shepherd
My Shield
My Song
Our Passover Lamb
Purifier
Refuge from The Storm
Rock of My Refuge

Rock of My Salvation
Rock of My Strength
Sanctifier
Savior
Shelter
Shepherd
Shield
Son of God
Strength
Strong Tower
Teacher
The Beginning and The End
The Bridegroom
The Comforter
The Door
The Godhead
The Last Adam
The Most High
The True Vine
Wonderful Counselor

The Names of God in the Old Testament

Name	Meaning	Reference
Adonai	Lord, Master	Genesis 15: 1-2
Elohim	God	Genesis 1:1; Psalm 19:1
El Elyon	The Most High God	Genesis 14:17-20; Isaiah 14:13-14
El Olam	The Everlasting God	Isaiah 40:28-31
El Shaddai	God Almighty	Genesis 17:1; Psalm 91:1
Jehovah-Gmolah	The Lord My Recompense	Jeremiah 51:6
Jehovah-Jireh	The Lord Will Provide	Genesis 22:13-14
Jehovah-Mekoddishkem	The Lord My Sanctifier	Exodus 31:13
Jehovah-Nissi	The Lord My Banner	Exodus 17:15
Jehovah-Rapha	The Lord that Heals	Exodus 15:26
Jehovah-Rohi	The Lord My Shephard	Psalm 23:1
Jehovah-Sabaoth	The Lord of Hosts	Isaiah 6:1-3
Jehovah-Shalom	The Lord is Peace	Judges 6:24
Jehovah-Shammah	The Lord Who is Present	Ezekiel 48:35
Jehovah-Tsidkenu	The Lord My Righteousness	Jeremiah 23:6
Yahweh	Lord, Jehovah	

Binding and Loosing

There is authority in the name of Jesus alone, for He spoke to His disciples in Matthew 28:18, saying, "...all power is given unto me in heaven and in earth". He then delegated that power to every blood-washed believer. He said, "I will give you the keys to the kingdom of heaven; whatever you bind on earth will be bound in heaven, and whatever you loose on earth will be loosed in heaven". Keys are practically used for locking and unlocking, opening and closing, and allowing or prohibiting. This, in turn, could result in obtainment or loss, freedom or bondage, or life or death. Jesus said, in Mark 16:17-18, "These signs will accompany those that believe: in My name they will cast out demons, they will speak with new tongues, they will pick up serpents, and, if they drink any deadly poison, it will not hurt them, they will lay hands on the sick, and they will recover".

When we "bind" something, or forbid it on earth, we're bringing out the will of God in the situation. When we "loose" something, or allow it on earth, we're fulfilling God's eternal purpose.

In the name of Jesus, we have legal authority to bind the works of darkness.

Bind:

☐ confine

☐ restrain

☐ restrict

☐ constrain with legal authority

☐ arrest

☐ apprehend

☐ handcuff

☐ lead captive

☐ take charge of

☐ lock up

☐ put to a stop

☐ muzzle

Loose:

☐ untie

☐ set free

☐ detach

☐ separate

☐ unhitch

☐ release

☐ unlock

☐ liberate

☐ disconnect

☐ unbind

☐ permit

☐ allow

Works of Darkness: (Ephesians 5:11)

☐ Sin	☐ Impurity	☐ Perversion	☐ Sickness
☐ Infirmity	☐ Death	☐ Destruction	☐ Curses
☐ Witchcraft	☐ Sorcery	☐ Divination	☐ Poverty
☐ Strife	☐ Lust	☐ Pride	☐ Rebellion
☐ Fear	☐ Torment	☐ Confusion	☐ Fornication
☐ Covetousness	☐ Revelry	☐ Drunkenness	☐ Bitterness
☐ Rage	☐ Slander	☐ Sexual Immorality	☐ Greed, etc.

For example, you could pray:

In the name of Jesus, I bind (restrict/disallow) fear, and I loose (permit/release) the perfect love of Christ to drive out every bit of fear. Father, You haven't given me a spirit of fear but love, power and a sound mind. I declare I will not fear because I have been made perfect in love (1 John 4:18; 2 Timothy 1:7).

About the Author

RAMONA LEWIS-FREEMAN is a Kingdom-builder who intercedes on the behalf of others. She hopes to encourage others to build a faith-filled prayer life. She has overcome by confessing and believing the Word of God through life's trials, tribulations, and hardships. She truly believes prayer is a vital factor in building a relationship with Christ. She's also the founder of the "I am ME" Women's Empowerment Group. Her mission is to empower, encourage, and inspire women of all ages to reach their greatest potential and become the best they can be in Christ. Ramona currently resides in Shreveport, Louisiana with her husband, Joshua Freeman, and their four beautiful children: Angel, Zaccheaus, Caleb, and Ethan. She's a friend, sibling, mentor, prayer warrior, and sounding board to many. She hopes to be a living example of Christ by continuing His works until His return.

Also Available from
J. Kenkade Publishing

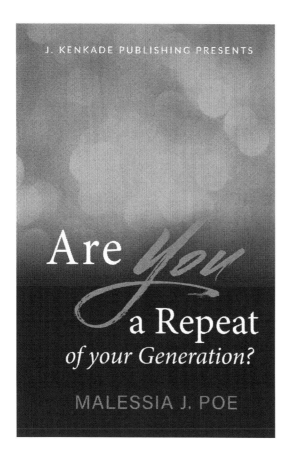

ISBN: 978-1-944486-36-5
Purchase at www.jkenkadepublishing.com

Have you been sabotaged? Are you the victim of a generational curse? Have you ever wondered, "Why am I here? Why do cycles repeat themselves in my life?" There is a hidden assassination attempt on your life by the enemy. However, God is a concerned God who wants to bring us into the full development and knowledge of who we are. The experiences we have in life shape us for better or worse. God wants us to stand steadfast in the liberty he has given us and root our identities in Him. It's time to move forward and break the cycle!

Also Available from
J. Kenkade Publishing

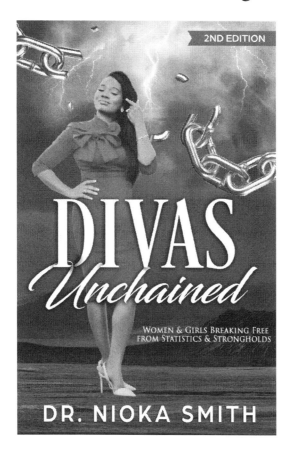

Also Available from
J. Kenkade Publishing

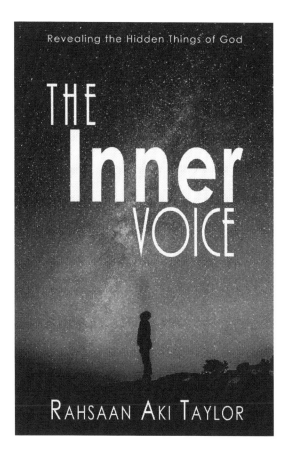

ISBN: 978-1-944486-12-9
Purchase at www.jkenkadepublishing.com

We all have wondered why bad things happen to us or someone we love. Often times, we never receive the answer to the questions that are asked. Therefore, the content of this book will expose the unknown. It is guaranteed to have you on the edge of your seat. It teaches how to prevent failures and mishaps and will reveal some of the hidden things of God.

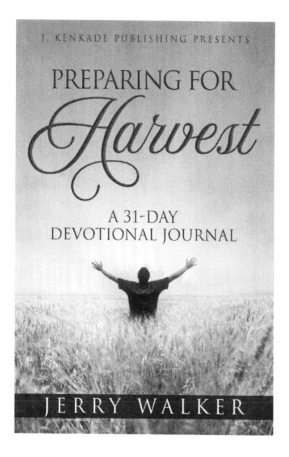

Made in the USA
Columbia, SC
04 March 2020